Gods of Sun
and
Sacrifice

AZTEC & MAYA MYTH

MYTH AND MANKIND

GODS OF SUN AND SACRIFICE: Aztec & Maya Myth
Writers: Tony Allan (The Mesoamerican World,
The People of Fire and Rain, Ritual and Belief,
The Mesoamerican Legacy), Tom Lowenstein
(Seven Macaw and the Hero Twins, Raising the Sky)
Consultant: Dr Tim Laughton

Created, edited and designed by
Duncan Baird Publishers
Castle House
75–76 Wells Street
London W1P 3RE

DUNCAN BAIRD PUBLISHERS
Managing Editor: Stephen Adamson
Managing Art Editor: Gabriella Le Grazie
Editors: Christina Rodenbeck, Peter Lewis
Designers: Gail Jones, Christine Keilty
Picture Researcher: Cecilia Weston-Baker
Artworks: Neil Gower
Map Artworks: Lorraine Harrison
Artwork Borders: Iona McGlashan
Editorial Researcher: Clare Richards
Editorial Assistant: Andrea Buzyn

TIME-LIFE BOOKS
Staff for GODS OF SUN AND SACRIFICE:
Aztec & Maya Myth
Editorial Manager: Tony Allan
Design Consultant: Mary Staples
Editorial Production: Justina Cox

Published by Time-Life Books BV, Amsterdam

First Time-Life English language printing 1997

TIME-LIFE is a trademark of
Time Warner Inc, USA

ISBN 0 7054 3543 1

Colour separation by Colourscan, Singapore
Printed and bound by Milanostampa, SpA, Farigliano, Italy

Title page: **Prisoners of war are sacrificed to the sun god. This Aztec codex was produced soon after the Spanish Conquest.**
Contents page: **A Classic Maya costume ornament made of shell and carved in the shape of a day-sign. The identity of the day-sign is uncertain but it may be one of the Hero Twins. From around AD600–800.**

30 29 28 27 26 25 24 23 22 21 20 19 18 17 16 15 14 13 12 11 10 9 8 7 6 5 4 3

Gods of Sun
and
Sacrifice

Contents

THE MESOAMERICAN WORLD

On November 7 1519, a battle-weary group of Spanish soldiers under the command of Hernán Cortés first caught sight of the Aztec capital, Tenochtitlan. Laid out on a complex of islands and causeways in the middle of a vast lake, it was a metropolis of some 200,000 people, twice the size of the largest European city of its day. "Those great towns and temples and buildings rising from the water, all made of stone, seemed like an enchanted vision," one of the Spanish conquistadors was later to write. "Indeed, some of our soldiers asked whether it was not all a dream … It was all so wonderful that I do not know how to describe this first glimpse of things never heard of, seen or dreamed of before."

What Cortés and his compatriots were gazing at was the culmination of 3,000 years of continuous cultural development. The Aztecs, who founded Tenochtitlan in 1325, were heirs to a tradition that began in the mid-second millennium BC with the Olmecs and was carried forward by a succession of peoples including the Zapotecs, Maya and Toltecs. Their imposing cities, temples and palaces resembled in many ways those of the ancient civilizations of Mesopotamia and Egypt. Yet unlike the cultures along the Nile and in the Fertile Crescent, Central American civilizations developed in almost total isolation from the rest of humankind and were subject to no cross-currents of influence from other cultures.

The tragic irony of the encounter in 1519 was that what the conquistadors marvelled at, they also came to destroy. The newcomers claimed the entire region for Christianity and the Spanish crown, and over the ensuing centuries its culture was reviled, its religion suppressed and its people seriously depleted by epidemic diseases and war.

Yet enough survived for later scholars to gain a fairly comprehensive understanding of the region's civilizations. The picture that emerges is one of beliefs and ways of thought that may, on occasion, bear some resemblance to contemporary attitudes, but in general are completely alien. To modern observers, ancient Central America has the enduring fascination of a culture that saw the world and man's role in it from an entirely different perspective.

Above: A 16th-century illustration shows Cortés's soldiers firing at envoys from the Aztec emperor Motecuhzoma.

Left: The Aztec capital of Tenochtitlan, pictured in early colonial times (*c.*1590). This print clearly shows how the city, in the centre of Lake Texcoco, was reached by causeways.

Early Central Americans

The first inhabitants of Central America were almost certainly descendants of immigrants from Siberia. No traces of the evolutionary precursors of *Homo sapiens* have been found anywhere in the Americas, leading scholars to conclude that the tribes who first populated them came from elsewhere. They most probably arrived over a land bridge that joined Alaska and Siberia across what is now the Bering Strait, when an ice age lowered the sea level between 15,000 and 35,000 years ago.

No one knows for certain when the initial settlers came, or at what date their descendants first migrated south to Mexico. Radiocarbon dating of bone fragments found near Mexico City indicates that the area was inhabited by around 21,000BC. These early Americans were hunter-gatherers; archaeologists have discovered traces of campfires and stone tools, along with the bones of the mammoths and mastodons that they killed and ate. By 5,000BC the inhabitants of the region had begun to develop farming techniques. Their crops were cultivated strains of plants that they had previously foraged in the wild, such as squash (pumpkin), chilli peppers, beans and avocado pears. They had also started to harvest a wild grass called teosinte that, over the centuries, was to have an enormous impact on the growth of Central American civilization; through selective breeding, the plant became the region's staple, maize.

Although the cultivation of foodstuffs began at roughly the same time in the New World as in the Old, the Central Americans faced certain difficulties that their counterparts in Europe and Asia did not have to contend with. Chief among these was a lack of beasts of burden. Without horses (or even the llamas used further south in the Andes), the inhabitants of the region had to rely on human effort to shift all loads. One consequence of this was that they never developed wheeled vehicles; although they were aware of the principle of the wheel, they evidently saw no benefit in putting it

Map of Mesoamerica, showing the various ancient cultures that flourished in the region, together with their principal sites.

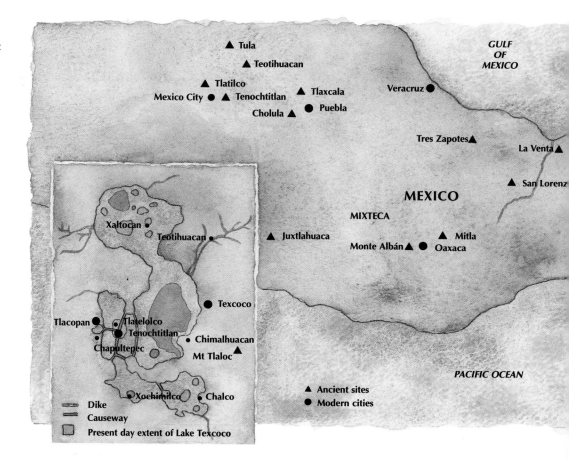

to use as a means of transportation. A second, related disadvantage was the absence of large domestic food animals. The Central Americans had no cows, pigs or sheep, and so relied on turkeys and small dogs – the latter were then regarded as fit for human consumption – to supplement the meat they obtained from hunting and fishing.

The areas of Central America where people settled also helped determine the kinds of civilizations that emerged there. The highlands of Mexico were traversed by mountain ranges that impeded

A merchant, pictured in a codex from the Postclassic Mixtec culture of Mexico, is wearing a backpack that contains a cargo of exotic quetzal birds, native to the Maya highlands. The brilliantly coloured feathers of the bird were highly prized and they were an important commodity throughout Mesoamerica. In the absence of pack animals, all loads were carried by people.

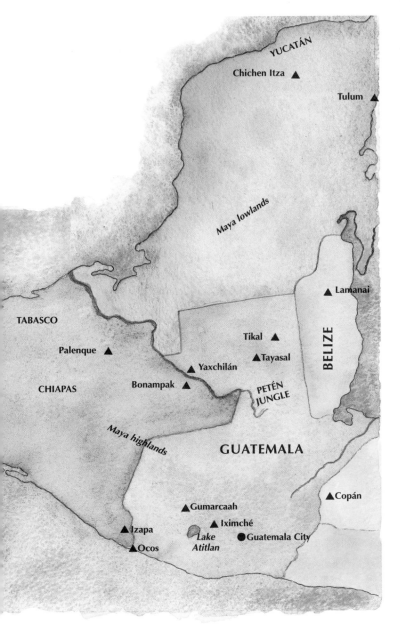

communication, so encouraging the growth of small kingdoms somewhat akin to the city-states of Ancient Greece. At the same time, the differences between the various regions stimulated cross-border trade to satisfy people's desire for goods that their own territories could not provide.

To the north lay the arid, sagebrush lands of the Mexican Plateau, which provided subsistence for nomadic tribes. Over the centuries, these itinerant groups posed a recurrent threat to the more settled communities whose borders they roamed.

A particularly desirable region was the Valley of Mexico, a fertile, 800,000-hectare basin with a temperate climate that lay 1,500 metres above sea level behind a protective barrier of mountains. This populous, well-irrigated area was to be the cradle of a succession of major cultures. Indeed, it retains its importance to this day, as the seat of government of the modern state of Mexico.

9

If the northern uplands formed one pole of civilization in the region, the other rose in much less favourable terrain in the southern jungle. The seat of Maya culture was the rainforest of the Yucatán peninsula in Mexico and the Petén ("flat region" in Mayan) in what is now northern Guatemala. Here, amid an exotic fauna of quetzal birds, jaguars and monkeys, the peoples of some twenty rival kingdoms cleared land for agriculture, cut drainage canals and built reservoirs, enabling the land to sustain population levels far in excess of the scant numbers living there nowadays.

Other areas of Central America remained untouched by early civilizations. In particular, the narrowest point of the American isthmus was largely unpopulated and unexplored. A band of virgin forest in present-day Costa Rica, Panama and northern Colombia cut the northern cultural centres off from the Andean civilizations some 2,000 kilometres to the south.

The term used by scholars for this Central American area of common heritage is Mesoamerica (literally "Middle America"), a word that has both geographical and chronological connotations. In terms of terrain, it describes the region that extends from the desert belt north of the Valley of Mexico through Guatemala and Honduras as far as western Nicaragua and Costa Rica (the southernmost point at which archaeological relics have been found). This region largely overlaps with what we now call Central America, but is not synonymous with it, since it excludes the whole of Panama and large tracts of other southern isthmus states, yet includes much of Mexico (categorized in geopolitical terms as part of North America). The timespan of Mesoamerican civilization stretches from the earliest traces of human habitation up to the Spanish Conquest in the sixteenth century.

In the millennia that followed the advent of agriculture, Mesoamerican peoples gradually abandoned their nomadic existence in favour of a more settled life in small villages. By c.2000BC, they had already begun to establish trade routes that were to remain in use even under the Spanish administration. The Central Americans of this period lived in huts of cane and thatch, made crude pottery, and modelled female figurines thought to represent a fertility goddess. Their tools included stone axes, flint knives and razor-sharp blades made from the glass-like volcanic rock called obsidian.

Birth of a Great Civilization

Then, around the middle of the second millennium BC, for reasons that remain obscure, culture began to flourish in an unlikely setting. On the banks of the sluggish rivers of the Gulf Coast jungles, large-scale monumental centres arose. At San Lorenzo, deep in the Veracruz rainforest, a 45-metre-high clay platform was constructed, surmounted by a cone-shaped clay mound and a series of courtyards. Beneath the complex ran the earliest known stone drainage system in the Americas. Fifty kilometres away, on the swampy island of La Venta, an earth pyramid 30 metres high dominated a ceremonial plaza.

The term "Olmec" has been coined to describe these first major Central American cultures; it was adapted from the Aztec word for the rubber-producing country where the sites were located. Even before extensive archaeological excavation began, artefacts came to light indicating that their inhabitants had made advances in the arts. In addition to elegant, enigmatic pieces fashioned from jade and serpentine, megalithic blocks were found, decorated with fantastic human and animal shapes.

The most surprising of all discoveries at these sites was a series of monumental heads; to date, seventeen have been found, standing between 1.6 and 3 metres high. Great effort clearly went into their creation. Those at San Lorenzo were carved from rock from the Tuxtla Mountains, 80 kilometres to the north. Huge boulders must have been dragged down from the heights, then transported by raft on a perilous river and sea journey.

From their heartland on the Gulf Coast, the Olmecs' influence extended over a huge area.

Graves containing Olmec-style objects have been excavated as far north as Mexico City, while rock carvings recalling Olmec motifs have been found in El Salvador, 1,200 kilometres to the south. But there is no firm evidence of an Olmec empire, and the entire civilization eventually disappeared. For reasons unknown, San Lorenzo was destroyed in about 900BC and La Venta followed some 500 years later. In each case, cultural objects were

deliberately defaced, then ritually buried. The legacy bequeathed to later cultures by the Olmecs has led them to be regarded as the region's parent civilization. Such enduring and diverse elements of Mesoamerican life as human sacrifice, bloodletting, pilgrimages, cave rituals, ceremonial centres with pyramids and spacious plazas, a concern with astronomy and the division of the world into four "directions" all have their origin in Olmec culture.

It is also believed that the Olmecs invented the first Mesoamerican writing system; over 180 symbols that may have served as glyphs have been identified on their works of art. However, this

This temple pyramid is situated at Monte Albán in central Mexico, the principal site of the Zapotecs. Monte Albán was settled between 600BC and AD750.

distinction also is claimed for the Zapotecs, who created a hitherto undeciphered script in order to record names and events. The Zapotecs are known from several sites in the Oaxaca Valley, the most important of which was Monte Albán, near the modern Mexican city of Oaxaca and less than 200 kilometres from the Olmec homeland. Although they were influenced by the earlier civilization, they had a distinct identity of their own.

Monte Albán was to prove one of the more long-lived Mesoamerican centres, serving as the Zapotec capital for well over a millennium. Its site was spectacular: 400 metres above the surrounding countryside stood an acropolis that extended for one kilometre, built on a levelled mountaintop and adorned with temples, terraces, courtyards and low stone pyramids. The materials for its construction must have been brought up from the valley, along with all the site's water, for no springs or wells have been found on the heights. This indicates that Monte Albán was a place of residence solely for the religious and political elite, serviced by the majority of the city's population, who lived in the valley below.

Monte Albán was laid out in the middle of the first millennium BC. By about AD200, Zapotec power was at its zenith, though it never extended far. It flourished for another 500 years, then apparently fell into decline. By AD900, the tombs of the Zapotec rulers of Monte Albán were being cleared

This bone carving depicts a Maya dignitary dressed in rich garments. The ancient civilization of the Maya was the most advanced in Mesoamerica.

TIMELINE OF MESOAMERICAN HISTORY

FORMATIVE PERIOD 2000–100BC

*c.*2000BC The use of pottery spreads in Mesoamerica, indicating settled village life

*c.*1800BC First Maya villages develop near the Pacific littoral

*c.*1200BC Earliest known Olmec centre flourishes at San Lorenzo

*c.*1100BC Building begins at the Olmec centre of La Venta

*c.*900BC San Lorenzo is destroyed

*c.*800BC Earliest known lowland Maya villages are established

An Olmec sculpture discovered in 1959

*c.*600–400BC Early Maya temples built at Nakte

*c.*500BC Zapotecs establish ceremonial centre at Monte Albán

*c.*400BC La Venta destroyed. Cuicuilco in Valley of Mexico develops into an important centre

*c.*100BC Tres Zapotes flourishes

PROTOCLASSIC PERIOD 100BC–AD300

*c.*100–50BC Maya temples built at Tikal and Uaxactun

36BC First known Long Count inscription: Chiopa de Lorzo Stela 2

*c.*AD50 Teotihuacan founded

*c.*200 Zapotec power is at its zenith

CLASSIC PERIOD AD300–900

*c.*350 Teotihuacan develops into the greatest city of Mesoamerica

of their contents and reused to house the remains of warriors of the conquering Mixtec race.

Lords of the Southern Jungle

Around the same period that the Zapotecs were flourishing, the Maya were creating a civilization in the jungles to the east. The history of this remarkable people has only emerged since the 1970s, as scholars learned to read their complex system of writing. As a result, many earlier theories about the Maya have been discovered to be incorrect.

Early writers had painted a picture of a people ruled by priests, guided solely by astronomy and religion and worshipping

in magnificent ceremonial centres far from the villages where most of the population lived. The newly deciphered records, however, reveal a world of rival city-states in almost permanent conflict. Their abiding concerns were with kingship, politics and war.

This reappraisal in no way detracts from the impressive achievements of the Maya. Their places of habitation were remarkable feats of engineering; huge communal effort must have been exerted to clear tracts of dense jungle, build drainage canals and reservoirs to contain rainfall

A Mixtec codex displays the characteristic screenfold form of such manuscripts. Writing systems were developed by early Central American cultures, but only became truly sophisticated with the Maya.

*c.***400** Teotihuacan's influence spreads to Maya lands

*c.***700** Maya civilization at its height. Major new temples built at Tikal

*c.***700** Zapotec power in decline

*c.***750** Teotihuacan overthrown, starting a time of troubles in Mexico

*c.***800** Bonampak murals are painted

POSTCLASSIC PERIOD AD900–1535

*c.***900** Toltecs establish their capital at Tula

*c.***909** Last dated Long Count inscription, at Maya centre of Uaxactun at Toniná, Chiapas

A "chacmool" at Chichen Itza

*c.***950** Maya centres in lowland Mexico and Guatemala fall into decline

*c.***980** Possible Toltec contact with the Maya at Chichen Itza

*c.***1000** Mixtecs use Monte Albán as burial site for their kings

*c.***1020** Chief Eight Deer Ocelot Claw becomes Mixtec ruler

*c.***1050** Toltecs expand their empire over much of Mexico

*c.***1170** Tula is sacked by northern tribes

*c.***1200** Aztecs enter the Valley of Mexico

*c.***1220** Maya abandon Chichen Itza

*c.***1270** Mayapan founded. It becomes the principal city of Yucatán

*c.***1325** Aztecs found their capital city, Tenochtitlan

*c.***1428** Aztecs become principal power in the Valley of Mexico

*c.***1450** Mayapan destroyed

*c.***1487** Rededication of Great Temple of Tenochtitlan

*c.***1502** Motecuhzoma II ascends the Aztec throne

A contemporary view of the Conquest

*c.***1519** Spanish arrive in Mexico

*c.***1521** Tenochtitlan falls to Hernán Cortés

*c.***1535** Emperor Charles V of Spain establishes Viceroyalty of New Spain in what is now called Central America

13

and raise the level of fields to prevent flooding. The Maya used the limestone that lay beneath the forest floor to build complexes of temples, pyramids and palaces, all grouped around courtyards and plazas standing on raised eminences. Their ceremonial art was created not just in stone but also in paint, as the brilliantly coloured murals discovered in 1946 at Bonampak (see pages 54–55) have demonstrated.

Most significant of all the achievements of the Maya was their writing system, which, with its combination of phonetic elements and pictorial signs, was the most sophisticated in the ancient Americas. The Maya used it to record their myths and history on stone tablets and in codices – books of fig-bark paper (see pages 26–27).

Astronomical and mathematical learning was also advanced among the Maya; they charted planetary movements with great accuracy, and introduced the concept of zero possibly even before its first use by Hindu mathematicians.

The many Maya city-states were grouped in a loose system of alliances around dominant powers. Each city-state had its own ruling dynasty, and fighting between the different centres seems to have been widespread. Time and effort could be devoted to construction and warfare, for once the forest had been cleared and planted, the land proved to be amazingly fecund. One modern survey has estimated that an average Maya smallholder could have supported his entire family on just forty-eight days' work a year.

Splendours of the Classic Age

Meanwhile, a new power was rising in the Valley of Mexico. In around AD50, surveyors started laying out a new city to a grid plan. Teotihuacan, as the settlement was called, was to become Mesoamerica's first metropolis, eventually extending over an area of 23 square kilometres and housing up to 200,000 people.

The identity of the builders of Teotihuacan is unknown; historians refer to them simply as the Teotihuacanos. The city's name comes from the Aztecs, who in later times regarded its ruins with religious awe and dubbed the site, in their Nahuatl language, "The Place of the Gods". What is certain is that the Teotihuacanos were a cosmopolitan people. Archaeological investigation has revealed that a colony of Zapotecs lived in the city for many generations, fashioning pottery in the style of Monte Albán. The peaceful presence of foreigners suggests that Teotihuacan flourished on commerce

An early example of the complex Mayan writing system is this stone stela covered with glyphic inscriptions. It was discovered at the major lowland site of Tikal in modern-day Guatemala. Such stone carvings predate the four surviving codices in which the Maya recorded their ritual observances and prophecies.

as much as on war. Surviving artwork corroborates this view. Images of warriors are not prominent on the walls of the palaces and temples that lined the city's central axis, an interlinked sequence of courts and plazas stretching six kilometres and known to later peoples, who only saw it in ruins, as "The Avenue of the Dead".

In its heyday this central thoroughfare must have teemed with life. At one end stood the 60-metre high structure known to the Aztecs as the "Pyramid of the Moon". Its even larger companion, the "Pyramid of the Sun", lay just to the east of the avenue. This 65-metre-high, stepped edifice covered the same ground area as the Great Pyramid in Egypt. Like the Pyramid of the Moon, it may have had a small temple on its summit.

Away from the city centre, the artisans and craftsmen who formed the bulk of the population lived in cramped apartment blocks, each housing up to one hundred people. Often the occupants shared a trade. Two large compounds, for example, housed workers of obsidian, mined in the hills behind the city. Indeed, it is likely that the presence of this vital raw material was the reason for Teotihuacan's foundation; certainly, trade in obsidian objects led the city's economic expansion.

At its peak, in around AD500, Teotihuacan presided over an age of prosperity that historians have called the "Classic Period" of Mesoamerican

This turquoise mosaic pectoral ornament, in the form of a double-headed serpent, is the work of a Mixtec jeweller, and dates from the 15th century. Mixtec craftsmanship was highly prized; an entire enclave of artisans from this culture lived in the Aztec city of Tenochtitlan.

civilization. Merchants journeyed north onto the Mexican plateau and as far south as Guatemala, trading in ceramic jugs, vases and incense burners, as well as obsidian tools. They returned with jade, jaguar skins and cacao beans from the Petén jungle, turquoise and greenstone from western Mexico, and conch shells from the Pacific and Gulf coasts. An especially highly prized commodity was the bright plumage of the little quetzal bird; its green tailfeathers were used as ornaments.

A Time of Blood

The Classic Period came to an end with the destruction of Teotihuacan sometime in the seventh or eighth century AD. The grand staircase of the Pyramid of the Moon was hacked away, and the palaces along the Avenue of the Dead were gutted by fire. Waves of militant nomadic tribesmen descended on the Valley of Mexico from the north. Some were driven back, but in the power vacuum that followed the collapse of the region's

15

principal city, others settled and prospered. One such group were the Mixtecs, who established themselves in the Zapotecs' former capital at Monte Albán. In the centuries that followed they were to become famous as craftsmen as well as for their fighting skills. The work of Mixtec goldsmiths, potters and mosaic artists became renowned throughout Mexico and was later prized above all other artefacts by the Aztecs.

In the Valley of Mexico, the most significant of the immigrant peoples were the Toltecs. They settled at Tula, just north of the valley's rim, in about AD950. Over the next two centuries, the city grew to become Teotihuacan's successor in splendour and importance. Its population, which eventually swelled to over 30,000, was divided between the Toltecs and people whom they referred to as "nonoalca", denoting all those who did not speak their own Nahuatl language.

Like the Teotihuacanos before them, the Toltecs traded extensively, venturing as far as what is now the southwestern United States in search of turquoise. They may have influenced the people who built Chichen Itza on the Yucatán peninsula; it is thought that they eventually overran this city. Both at Chichen Itza and in their northern homeland, the Toltecs introduced a new and sinister martial note into Mesoamerican culture. Colossal images of soldiers supported their temples, whose walls were adorned with the emblems of warrior societies, such as jaguars, coyotes and eagles.

Human sacrifice, which had played a part in Mesoamerican society at least since Olmec times, now took on greater prominence. Skull-racks to display the heads of victims first appeared under the Toltecs. But perhaps their most distinctive and gruesome innovation was the "chacmool", a reclining stone figure holding a bowl on its stomach for displaying a plucked-out human heart.

In their obsession with sacrifice, and in many other respects, the Aztecs were the Toltecs' natural successors. Their culture arose during another of Mesoamerica's periodic power vacuums, after the Toltec city of Tula was destroyed in the twelfth century. At this time, the Aztecs were a band of nomads, who had arrived in the Valley of Mexico from the north only two centuries earlier.

When establishing their future capital of Tenochtitlan in 1345, they first hired themselves out as mercenaries to the rulers of various city-

These giant stone columns carved in the shape of warriors ready for battle surmount one of the pyramids at the Toltec site of Tula. Originally, they were brightly painted.

states (see page 99). Before long they were strong enough to make a bid for power in their own right, and by 1428 they had become the dominant force in the region. Aztec society thus became entirely geared towards success in war. In a world of small, competing kingdoms, all with access to similar arsenals of weapons, the Aztecs swiftly realized that supremacy was to be gained by the people with the most disciplined fighting forces.

Consequently, male children were brought up from birth on an ideology of combat; midwives present at the delivery of boys gave them miniature shields and arrows to symbolize their martial destiny, while the infants' umbilical cords were entrusted to warriors for burial on a battlefield.

Unsurprisingly, this profoundly militaristic society rapidly embarked on a programme of armed expansion. Their forces ranged across

An Extended Family of Gods

Although the different Mesoamerican cultures each had their own gods, these divinities often had many features in common.

Tlaloc and Chac, the ancient rain gods of central Mexico and the southeastern Maya lands respectively, shared many traits. Both appear on artefacts from as early as the first century BC.

The two gods were associated not just with rain but also with lightning and running water, especially mountain streams. They were helped by lesser divinities, known as tlaloques and chacs, that served as spirits of highlands and storms. In each case, four of these attendants were specifically identified with the four directions – north, south, east and west. These quartets of gods featured in slightly differing versions of a shared myth recounting how a mountain was cracked open to give maize to the human race.

Outwardly, the two were very different, although neither could be described as handsome. Tlaloc is easily identified in reliefs by his goggle eyes and prominent, jaguar-like teeth. Chac, in contrast, was initially depicted with antenna-like whiskers and a blunt snout, replaced in later images by a bulbous caricature of a nose.

An Aztec stone carving shows Tlaloc, the god of rain, as a fearsome snaggle-toothed creature.

17

The Aztec founding of Tenochtitlan was recorded in several texts. This version is from the *Codex Boturini*.

sacrificed in order to provide the sun with nourishment for its journey across the sky. The Aztecs believed that only fresh supplies of blood could ensure its safe passage.

The prosperity brought by the Aztecs' military and commercial activities turned their capital, Tenochtitlan, into one of the great cities of the sixteenth-century world. Its vast markets were full of merchandise from all over Mesoamerica, and its ceremonial plazas rivalled even those of Teotihuacan in size and magnificence. The royal palaces were surrounded by beautiful gardens, a huge aviary maintained by 300 keepers and a private zoo containing big cats, wolves and reptiles.

Yet for all its opulence the Aztec empire was built on unstable foundations. Its vassal states were temporarily subdued rather than permanently conquered, and their peoples resentfully awaited an opportunity to cast off the imperial yoke. Even close to home there were independent states that the Aztecs had failed to bring to heel. Bitter enemies of the imperial power, these pockets of resistance, such as the small state of Tlaxcala to the east of Tenochtitlan, were to prove valuable allies to the Spanish in their conquest of the Aztecs.

much of Mexico, building up an empire that occupied, by the turn of the fifteenth century, over 150,000 square kilometres – about the size of modern Italy. The Aztecs did not have enough men or resources to establish a permanent presence in the lands they conquered, so they demanded instead payment of an annual tribute, reinforcing their demand with the threat of renewed military action.

By no means all the Aztecs' battles were fought with economic ends in mind. After inheriting and refining the Toltec practice of human sacrifice, they needed a regular supply of prisoners-of-war to meet the demand for victims. To obtain them, they fought the so-called "Flower Wars" against rival states; the sole purpose of these campaigns was to take captives for the sacrificial altar. The justification for ritual execution was gained from myths that told how gods were once

A Common Heritage of Myth

In spite of their internecine rivalries, the various Central American peoples shared gods and myths almost as readily as they exchanged trade goods. While most nations had one or more deities exclusive to themselves, they also held other gods in common with their neighbours.

One important aspect of the collective heritage of the region was the sheer size of its pantheon. The Aztecs worshipped more than forty major deities, as well as dozens of lesser or local ones. Single gods were assigned to most natural phenomena – for example birth, death or springtime – while entire groups of deities were associated with maize, the alcoholic drink called pulque and the fertility of the Earth. As a further complexity, the Mesoamericans often twinned their gods, either by providing them with consorts who extended or enhanced their own field of action, or by splitting the attributes of a single deity into two or more manifestations. This tendency extended, in at least one case, to identifying an historical human figure with a god (see pages 122–23).

A distinctive and enduring preoccupation of Mesoamerican religion was the measurement of time; the earliest example of writing, from a Zapotec source of about 600BC, is a calendar notation. Both Aztec and Maya priests used two separate calendars, one of 365 and the other of 260 days, to predict the future and record the passing of the seasons. The symbolism of dates was further related to a concern with astronomy. Study of the stars was regarded as vital for an understanding of how they impinged on Earthly events.

However esoteric its theology, Mesoamerican religion also had a popular aspect, namely its emphasis on dramatic ritual and ceremony. Its temples, sited ostentatiously on top of pyramids, were designed to maintain a strict separation between priests and people, while at the same time placing religious ritual in full public view. By the time of the Spanish Conquest, many of these ceremonies included a human sacrifice.

The Aztecs probably offered up more sacrificial victims than any other people in recorded history. In this, they were enacting a Mesoamerican tradition that originated far back in the region's past. Yet immediate political concerns also played a major role; it is significant that ritual killing increased under the Toltecs and Aztecs, whose warrior aristocracies had a vested interest in sustaining the armed conflict that supplied the priesthood with victims.

At root, however, sacrifice fulfilled a deeply ingrained desire to preserve cosmic harmony and balance. Regular offerings of blood appeased the gods and ensured the continued motion of the universe. Underlying the pomp and splendour of Mesoamerican ritual was a mortal dread concerning the impermanence of the world and a profound pessimism about the human condition.

These miniature models of gods once occupied Aztec household shrines. In common with earlier Mesoamerican cultures, the Aztecs worshipped an extensive pantheon of gods, and religion pervaded all areas of life.

OLMEC SCULPTURES

Few of the world's art treasures conceal more mysteries than the stone sculptures of the Olmecs, the Gulf Coast people who created Mesoamerica's first civilization more than 3,000 years ago. The objects range from exquisite miniatures fashioned from jade and serpentine to colossal stone heads that may have represented early rulers. One feature that distinguishes them from the art of later peoples is their stark realism; many of the sculptures are fashioned in the round, portraying the human figure in squat but accurate detail. Almost nothing is known of the purposes for which they were made, although buried groups of figurines have been found arranged in detailed tableaux that must have had some ritual significance.

Above: This ornamental head, dating from the end of the Olmec era in about AD400-600, once adorned equipment used in an early version of the ritual ballgame that was a feature of most Mesoamerican cultures.

Above: This 23cm-high mask is made of jade, which was the most valued stone in Mesoamerica. Lacking metal tools, sculptors shaped it with implements made of the same tough material.

Right: The snarling mouth and cleft head of this jade figurine suggest that it represents a jaguar god. The V-shaped indentation in the forehead may be a stylized rendition of the distinctive furrow on the animal's skull.

Above: Almost two metres high, this monumental head is one of four found at La Venta, near the Gulf Coast. Scholars speculate that they may have portrayed rulers of the city.

Right: A standing man (*top*) and a terracotta crying baby (*bottom*) show the Olmec propensity for portraying the human body in the round. Groups of such figurines have been found buried ceremonially.

SEVEN MACAW AND THE HERO TWINS

The myths and beliefs of the Maya present an ambivalent picture. On the one hand, many of their preoccupations are shared with other Mesoamerican peoples, while on the other, the way in which these beliefs are articulated gives evidence of a profoundly original culture.

Maya mythology is preserved in a number of forms, chief among which is the *Popol Vuh*, a sacred manuscript of the Quiché people (see pages 28–29). Further sources include other codices dating from before the Spanish Conquest, and hieroglyphic inscriptions found on standing stones, temple walls and ceramic artefacts.

In common with other Mesoamerican societies, the Maya believed they inhabited a universe that was fundamentally unstable yet highly predictable. Within this rigidly structured cosmos, the human race and all other living creatures occupied preordained positions. The workings of this system were impersonal and implacable. Nothing could alter the patterns of origination and destruction, and the universe was thought already to have passed through a series of apocalyptic collapses and renewals. What was unique about the Maya expression of this widespread belief was the way in which it was underpinned by detailed mathematical and calendrical calculations. These were designed to determine the precise length of the cycles in which such momentous events recurred; the Maya reckoned each of these universal cycles to have a duration of thirteen *baktuns* (with one *baktun* equivalent to 400 years). Accordingly, the world and its inhabitants would be annihilated every 5,200 years. The most recent cycle began in 3114BC and is due to end on December 23 2012.

The centrepiece of the creation myth recounted in the *Popol Vuh* is the epic struggle between a monstrous bird deity known as Seven Macaw (Vucub Caquix), who set himself up as a false sun before the dawn of time, and two heroes, the twins Hunahpu and Xbalanque. Once this early pretender to power and his offspring had been killed, humans could be created.

Above: The pyramid called Temple I at Tikal has nine giant steps, symbolizing the levels of the Maya Underworld.

Left: Lady Xoc lets blood, while her husband King Shield Jaguar holds a torch over her. His headdress includes the head of a sacrificial victim. Glyphs record the date of this ritual as October 28 709.

23

The Maya Universe

The Maya thought of the universe as having a tripartite structure, arranged in strata. The uppermost layer of existence was Heaven. Below this lay the Earth (see pages 30–31), while the lowest level comprised a fearsome Underworld.

In the cosmology of the Maya, Heaven was a realm of permanence; its stability was assured by massive cosmic trees that anchored it firmly in place. This sphere of existence was divided into thirteen distinct levels, each of which was presided over by a god. The Maya believed that a person had to have met a violent end if they were to enter Heaven in the afterlife. Each stratum was reserved for a particular kind of violent death; thus, sacrificial victims inhabited a layer of their own, while those who had been struck by lightning or drowned resided in the level that was ruled by the rain god Chac.

So deeply ingrained was this conception of a stratified universe among the Maya that their temples and shrines were most commonly built on top of pyramids or on the summits of mountains, in order that religious observances and rituals could be conducted as close as humanly possible to the divine realms of the sky.

At the base of the cosmic structure lay the gloomy Underworld kingdom that was known to the Quiché Maya as Xibalba ("place of fright"). This realm was made up of nine layers and had its own complement of deities. One god particularly identified with the Underworld was the screech-owl Muan, who was also associated with maize and rain. In many cases the Underworld gods resembled, or represented certain aspects of, deities of the Earth and sky.

Xibalba was the destination of the great majority of people after their death. In all Meso-american societies, no notion of human morality was attached to the afterlife; unlike Hell in Christian cosmology, the Maya Underworld was not reserved for sinners, but was simply the final home of everyone who had not come to a violent end. Thus it was that kings, priests and noblemen

One of a number of gods constantly revered in the Maya pantheon was the Old Fire God, as depicted in this effigy from Tikal. The Old Fire God was one of the oldest deities of Mesoamerican civilizations.

who passed away peacefully were interred in imposing nine-layer pyramids – such as Temple I at Tikal, the Castillo at Chichen Itza (see pages 80–81), and the Temple of Inscriptions at Palenque – which symbolized the levels of Xibalba.

Once a person had entered the Underworld, they were faced with a series of trials in which they were required to outwit the repellent gods who held sway over this realm. If victorious, the deceased person would ultimately ascend into the sky as a heavenly body. For the Maya, the epitome of how to negotiate the ordeals of the Underworld successfully was the conduct of the Hero Twins, who thwarted the Lords of Xibalba at every twist and turn (see pages 40–45).

The Maya worshipped an extensive pantheon of deities. These are extremely difficult to categorize, as many gods appeared in a number of guises. For example, a particular deity might possess male and female characteristics, and have the capacity to be both old and young, and to assume either spiritual or corporeal form. In addition, many supernatural beings displayed animal characteristics, or combined human and divine attributes. Thus, the Hero Twins of the *Popol Vuh,* who left the upper world and descended into the depths to subdue the lords of the Underworld, were themselves demigods.

Similar confusion surrounds the question of the supreme god of the Maya. At the beginning of Maya civilization (the Formative period), two major deities, Itzamna (the god of writing, curing and divination, who was also known as Hunab Ku, or "Only Spirit") and Seven Macaw, occupied this position at various times. Later, during the period known as the Preclassic, Seven Macaw rose to prominence as the "Principal Bird Deity" and was thought to exert a powerful and benign influence over people's lives. By the time the *Popol Vuh* of the Quiché Maya came to be written, however, he had been reduced to the role of a boastful impostor. For their part, the Quiché Maya revered a patron deity called Tohil (see page 47) as the Supreme Being, while the Postclassic period witnessed the growth of cults to central Mexican

gods such as the Plumed Serpent, Quetzalcoatl. Likewise, the agricultural deity Xipe Totec ("Our Lord the Flayed One") had gained a large cult following by the time of the Spanish Conquest.

While the identity of the highest deity thus changed over time, other long-established deities in the Maya pantheon, such as the rain god Chac and the Maize God (who corresponded to the divine hero One Hunahpu), were consistently revered. The trees that held the cosmos in place at its four corners, together with a central World Tree, were common features of the mythology and religion of several Mesoamerican cultures. The *Books*

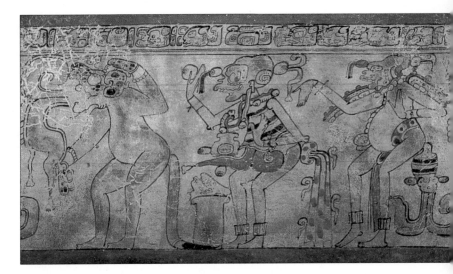

The putrid Lords of Xibalba cavort along the side of this ceramic pot. The figure on the left is feline; from its mouth issues a graphic depiction of halitosis. The central lord has a ghastly, fleshless skull, while the figure on the right has a stomach distended by parasitic disease and grotesque insect-like wings on its shoulders.

of Chilam Balam (see page 27) describe the establishment of the trees aligned to the four cardinal directions as the first act of creation following the destruction of the old cosmos. Every tree and direction had its own colour – white for north, yellow for south, red for east and black for west, while the central tree was green. Similarly, all the birds and plants associated with each tree were of the same colour.

25

The Sacred Texts

Mayan writing, which has only begun to be deciphered in the past twenty to thirty years, was a highly developed system of ideographs and phonetics. The earliest hieroglyphic inscriptions were made on temple walls, but later came to be written down in sacred books. Such texts recorded religious ritual in far greater detail than was possible in stone.

The writing system of the Maya, which was formulated in the Late Preclassic period (300BC–AD100), may have originated in the Pacific highland areas of Chiapas and Guatemala around 100BC to AD100. Here, hieroglyphic inscriptions that have much in common with later Mayan script have been discovered on stone stelae. Throughout the Early Classic and Late Classic periods (AD600–900), the Maya recorded ritual, calendrical and historical information on their temple pyramids and other grand public buildings.

These books were composed of long strips either of paper made from the bark of fig trees or of deer hide. They were folded in the manner of a screen, and then coated with a fine layer of white lime-based plaster (gesso). On this base, images were drawn in brilliantly coloured inks, usually depicting seated or standing gods wearing elaborate headdresses, together with rows of hieroglyphic symbols representing each deity's name and epithets. Despite the preponderance of such images, however, pre-contact codices contain little in the way of sustained mythological narrative. Rather, they focus on elaborate calendrical cycles as a way of divining the future (see pages 114–117); most of their prophecies relate to agricultural matters. In all codices, both sides of the manuscript were used and they were always read from left to right.

The Codices Destroyed

Many thousands of these codices must have been produced, but most fell prey to the religious fervour of the Spanish early in the sixteenth century. Only three books of the ancient Maya were originally thought to have survived. These are known as the Madrid, Paris and Dresden codices, and date from the Postclassic and early Colonial periods. Post-colonial codices almost always show the influence of the Spanish. Remarkably, a

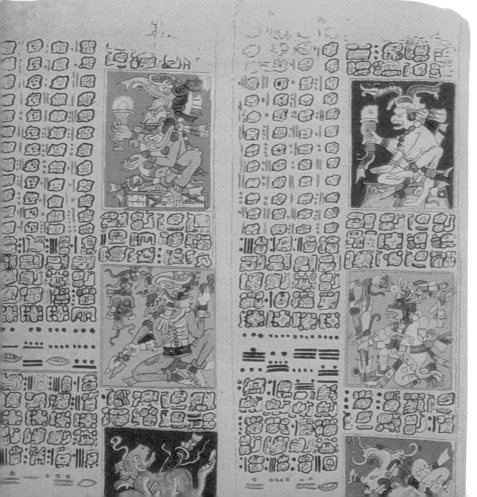

The *Dresden Codex* – so called because it is preserved in the Sächsische Landesbibliothek in Dresden, Germany – is the most complete of all the surviving Maya codices. It is especially noteworthy for its extraordinarily accurate calculations of the movements of the planet Venus, shown here.

Maya Views of the Conquest

Two Maya chronicles give eyewitness testimony of the cataclysmic change that occurred with the invasion of the Spanish. One – the Annals of the Cakchiquels – is from the southern highlands, while the other is a series of documents from the Yucatán known as the Books of Chilam Balam.

The Cakchiquels were close neighbours and rivals of the Quiché, inhabiting a settlement called Iximché near Lake Atitlan. Survivors of the Spanish Conquest of the region in 1523–24 transcribed an account of local history from hieroglyphs into an alphabetic system. This chronicle – the *Annals of the Cakchiquels* – ran from the mythic origins of the people up to contemporary times, and was continuously added to until 1604. The work lucidly documents momentous events, and gives an even-handed account of the invasion, criticizing Spanish brutality yet praising acts of clemency.

The *Books of Chilam Balam* of the Yucatec Maya contain a mixture of history, myth and prophecy. Kept by the nobles of individual communities from the early sixteenth century onwards, these books were recopied and added to until the nineteenth century. They take their title (literally, "Jaguar Translator") from the name of a seer who had prophesied the Spanish invasion and cultural hegemony. The text relates how he foresaw the violent arrival of "bearded men of the east" and even predicted the cultural assimilation of the Maya people: "You will be brothers-in-law to the invaders, and you will wear their clothing and their hats, and speak their language."

A page from the *Book of Chilam Balam*, showing the Maya months. The text is in Mayan, written in a Roman alphabet; the ancient glyphs alongside are pure decoration.

fourth work – the *Grolier Codex* – lay undiscovered in a cave in southwestern Maya territory until the early 1970s. Written in the Toltec-Maya style, it consists of a few pages of detailed astronomical calculations in tabular form and is believed to date from the thirteenth century.

The oldest and most lavishly illustrated pre-Conquest text – the *Dresden Codex* from Post-classic Yucatán – is thought to have been sent among a number of other documents to the Holy Roman Emperor Charles V of Spain by Hernán Cortés early in the sixteenth century. It has survived against all odds, since the first Catholic bishop to be appointed to the Yucatán region, Diego de Landa, was a religious zealot who destroyed the sacred books of the indigenous people. In Landa's own words: "We found a great number of books in these letters of theirs, and because they contained nothing but superstition and the devil's falsehoods, we burned them all."

A Rich Source of Myth

The southern Maya who inhabited the valleys of highland Guatemala were, in fact, several separate nations. The most powerful of these was the kingdom of the Quiché, a tough, resourceful people whose original homeland was to the west in Mexico. In the highlands, the Quiché expanded rapidly during the fifteenth century, developing a sophisticated culture based around fortified sites. Their most important sacred text to survive the Spanish Conquest – the *Popol Vuh*, or "council book" – is a mixture of myth and history that explains the origins of the Quiché people.

The *Popol Vuh* differs from the other Maya codices in containing a wealth of religious narrative. The work divides into three sections: the creation of the Earth and the initial (ultimately abortive) attempts to fashion its first inhabitants; the legend of the Hero Twins and their antecedents; and finally the successful creation of human beings. Within the last section is included a history of the

founding and succession of the Quiché dynasties, a chronicle that continues beyond the arrival of the Spanish conquistadors in 1523–24.

The identity of the author of the first *Popol Vuh* – a hieroglyphic book – is not known. The form in which the text has come down to the present day is as a transcription into the Roman alphabet of the original Maya glyphs. This endeavour is

thought to have been embarked upon by members of three branches of the Quiché elite in the mid-sixteenth century. Undertaken in defiance of the suppression of Maya culture by the Spanish invaders, the secret task of reconstructing the *Popol Vuh* represented a conscious desire to preserve the sacred text for posterity. By the time the work fell into the hands of the Spanish later in the century, the book-burning zeal of the Inquisition had abated, and so the *Popol Vuh* was preserved as an historical curio.

In around 1703, a Quiché-speaking Franciscan friar called Francisco Ximenez chanced upon a manuscript of the alphabetic *Popol Vuh* in the settlement of Chichicastenango on the shores of Lake Atitlan where he was the parish priest. Ximenez copied the Quiché text and made his own parallel translation into Spanish. This is now the earliest surviving version of the *Popol Vuh*. Ximenez's manuscript remained in the keeping of the Roman Catholic authorities for more than a century. Thereafter, it passed into the possession of the University of San Carlos in Guatemala City.

In the mid-nineteenth century, two foreign scholars working independently of one another became interested in the text. An Austrian physician, Carl Scherzer, who first discovered the work in 1854, published Ximenez's Spanish translation in Vienna three years later. Then, in 1861, a French priest, Charles Etienne Brasseur, purchased the manuscript and brought it back to Paris, where he published the Quiché text alongside a parallel translation into his native language. By the early years of the twentieth century, Ximenez's copy of the *Popol Vuh* had arrived at its current home, the Newberry Library in Chicago, a renowned centre for Native American studies.

Left: A page of the parallel translation of the *Popol Vuh* by Francisco Ximenez.

Below: A Maya vase depicting a turkey and a dog; Maya mythology, such as that contained in the *Popol Vuh*, abounds in stories concerning animals.

A view of Lake Atitlan in the Guatemala highlands, looking towards three volcanoes situated on the south shore. On this lake lies the town of Chichicastenango, where the Quiché Maya *Popol Vuh* was discovered in the early 18th century.

29

The Earth is Born

The *Popol Vuh* opens with a description of how the gods from two distinct realms – the sea and the sky – joined forces to create the world in its present form. This momentous event took place amid great stillness and was the result of language: when the creator gods whispered the word Earth, the Earth came into being. According to Maya calculations creation took place recently – at the beginning of the current universal cycle, in 3114BC.

Prior to the act of creation, there was a dark void, containing nothing except the sky and the sea. There were no rocks, meadows or forests, nor were there any people, animals, fish or birds. Yet great creative potential was latent in this emptiness, in the shape of several gods who resided either in the sea or the sky.

Eventually, two of the principal deities, one from each realm, joined together to instigate creation. The sky god creator was called Heart of Sky, or Hurricane, and manifested himself as lightning. His partner was a sea god known as Sovereign Plumed Serpent, or Gucumatz. According to the *Popol Vuh*, these two deities were "great knowers and thinkers", and life began as soon as they engaged in dialogue.

The gods' first task – to shape the Earth from the vast and silent waters – is compared to the way that a farmer prepares a field of maize.

The importance of maize to the Maya was signified by the numerous gods associated with it. This statue of a maize god is from Honduras.

This agricultural metaphor anticipates the gods' long-term plan to create the present human race, or "people of corn".

The gods professed themselves happy with their work. The waters had receded, mountains arisen and trees grown. Over their new creation stood the vault of the sky. However, the Earth's silence still troubled them. Clearly, they needed to create animals. So they brought to life deer, birds, jaguars and serpents and assigned them their places in the forest.

Believing that these creatures would naturally have the power of speech, the gods told them to announce themselves. But the only noises that they could utter were inarticulate screeches, grunts, howls and bellows. This greatly displeased the gods, because they had failed to fashion creatures who could pay them the respect that they felt was due. In their anger and disappointment, the gods ordered the animals never to stray beyond the limits of the forest and to be subservient to the human beings who were to come.

Mud People and Wooden People

In Maya mythology, there is no sovereign deity who makes perfect beings in its own image. Rather, before humans arrived on the scene, the creator gods attempted several times to people the world with beings who could reflect their glory. When these proved inadequate, they were obliged to destroy them and try again.

Disappointed that the animals – their first animate creations – did not speak a comprehensible language, Gucumatz and Hurricane decided to create another species. What they required on Earth were beings who could call on them by name, pay them homage and feed them with regular sacrifices.

Thus they set about fashioning bodies out of earth and mud. But no sooner were they made than the creatures seemed utterly wrong; they were too soft and fell to pieces easily, their faces were lopsided and they could not articulate their words properly. Moreover, these mud people had no conception of how to honour the gods by assigning them particular days of worship within a calendar. In the absence of this, no proper relationship could be established between the divine beings and their creations.

The gods then tried for a second time. On this occasion, they made people out of wood. The males were hewn from the wood of the coral tree, while the females were made out of the fibrous cores of bulrushes. At first, these wooden people seemed to be a success. Their appearance and language were correct, and they were able to procreate. But two major defects soon became apparent. Firstly, their minds were devoid of thoughts and their hearts were empty of feelings; as a result, they had no memory of or devotion to their creators. Secondly, they did not develop physically. Their skin was dry and crusty, their movements uncoordinated and their bodies were wont to warp.

So Hurricane called forth a mighty flood and drowned the wooden manikins. The only reminders of these prototype people, according to Maya belief, are the forest monkeys, who resemble underdeveloped humans.

The First Genocide

The *Popol Vuh* and other Mayan texts contain graphic portrayals of how Hurricane brutally exterminated the race of wooden people that he and his fellow creator god Gucumatz had made. After a flood had accounted for most of the people, Hurricane visited a series of gruesome fates upon the survivors.

To rid himself of the last of his failed creations, Hurricane first called on the services of two fearsome monsters: one, called Gouger of Faces, plucked out the wooden people's eyes, while the other – Sudden Bloodletter – ripped off their heads. In addition, the help of two monstrous jaguars, known as Crunching Jaguar and Tearing Jaguar, was enlisted; they tore people limb from limb and ate their flesh.

Pictorial Maya codices show in gory detail some of the results of unleashing these monsters. For example, in the *Madrid Codex*, Gouger of Faces is portrayed as a king vulture diving on a seated wooden manikin. In its beak, the monstrous bird holds one of its victim's eyes, which remains attached to its socket by the optic nerve.

The *Popol Vuh*, though lacking in illustrations, gives a vivid description of the holocaust that overtook the wooden people. It relates how molten pitch rained down from the sky onto them, and how they were then crushed and hammered, until their flesh and bones were reduced to dust. The text goes on to tell how survivors were relentlessly hunted down in a permanent nightmarish twilight where rain falls incessantly. All the

A fearsome animal lurks on the far left of this detail of a page from the *Madrid Codex* – also known as the *Codex Tro-Cortesianus*. This and the other surviving pictorial Maya codices contain many depictions of the dreadful beasts which were let loose by the creator gods Hurricane and Gucumatz to eradicate the inadequate wooden people they created.

accounts and images of this genocide in the codices bear witness to the sheer fury of the gods' attack on their flawed creations for their dullness and incompetence.

The onslaught continued unabated. Animals burst into people's houses, bringing wild nature into what had been domestic calm. The belief persists in modern Maya society that wild animals or birds which suddenly irrupt into a human dwelling are a warning of the gods' displeasure.

Domestic Chaos

Then new heights of terror were reached as the natural order was turned completely upside down. While the wild animals burst into the wooden people's homes, their possessions – animate and inanimate – began to speak. The domestic animals, such as dogs and turkeys, rebuked their former masters for having mistreated and eaten them. In a horribly violent image, the dogs proclaimed their revenge, snapping out that "today you people will taste the teeth in our mouths! We shall eat you instead!"

Likewise, the previously dumb, inanimate kitchen equipment came to life. Water jars, grinding stones and tortilla griddles all sprang into action. The grinding stones complained how their faces had been ripped and rubbed all day. "At first," announced the stones, "we did you service. But now the boot's on the other foot!" As they said this, they joined Hurricane in pounding the wooden people to dust.

The cooking pots then took up the theme, upbraiding the people for constantly scorching their faces and making their mouths sooty. "In return," they declared, "we shall burn you!" Finally, even the hearth stones came flying right out of the fireplace, like stones shooting out of a volcano, and rained down upon the wooden people's heads, crushing their faces.

Dogs were an integral part of every Maya household; as well as guarding the property, they made a tasty meal for the family every now and then. This vessel in the shape of a dog may have been used ritually.

In the face of this fearsome attack, the wooden people ran for their lives in all directions. Some climbed on to the roofs of their houses, but these structures gave way and collapsed. Those who clambered up into the trees to escape the terrifying onslaught were instantly shaken down to the ground by the branches themselves. Others rushed to seek shelter in caves, only to see huge boulders roll into the cave entrances behind them, entombing them forever. Thus the fate of the unfortunate wooden people was sealed and their destruction was complete.

The Arrogant Impostor

Prior to the dawning of the present era, a monstrous bird known as Seven Macaw (Mayan: Vucub Caquix) set himself up as the principal deity presiding over the gloomy twilight world that was left behind after the universal flood. This presumptuous monster and his vain offspring had to be destroyed before the human race could be created.

Seven Macaw was characterized above all by his boastfulness and arrogance, and the way that he basked in his own delusions of grandeur. Chief among these was his claim to be both the sun and the moon. At this early stage, night and day had not yet become separate. Instead, a kind of "sun–moon" shone dimly through a mantel of cloud, creating a state of permanent twilight.

This Classic period tripod vase depicts the bird deity Seven Macaw, or Vucub Caquix. The bird is shown in characteristically proud posture, with its wings outstretched and wearing a necklace which is thought to signify power.

In these crepuscular conditions, Seven Macaw was far and away the brightest being. "My light is great," he crowed, "I glow, I glitter, I shine." And, indeed, his physical appearance was nothing short of spectacular. His splendid plumage was made of precious metals and gemstones. His face was framed by jewel-encrusted, burnished metal plates, while his teeth were gleaming blue sapphires. Even the nest he lived in was built of dazzling metal. His proud boast was that his great white beak "shone into the distance like the moon".

Seven Macaw's vainglory even extended to claiming that he had dominion over time, since he fancied that he represented all the days and months of the year. His two sons entertained similar conceits: Zipacna dubbed himself the "maker of mountains", while Earthquake believed that he had the power to "bring down the sky". Yet in the very arrogance of these beings lay the seeds of their own destruction, for such exorbitant claims constituted a direct challenge to the authority of the founder gods (see pages 30–33). Clearly, this family of monsters would have to be done away with and more modest beings created in their place if the gods were to receive the respect they demanded.

Accordingly, Seven Macaw and his sons were engaged in combat by the Hero Twins Hunahpu and Xbalanque. These important characters appear in the *Popol Vuh* as the offspring of the union between the god Hun Hunahpu ("One Hunahpu") and an Underworld maiden known as Xquic ("Blood Moon"). Their brave exploits, which they undertake in order to avenge the death of their father and his brother in the Underworld, all centre on vanquishing the evil forces that ruled the early world and on preparing the ground for the advent of human beings.

The first confrontation between Seven Macaw and the Hero Twins is described in terms of a hunting expedition. First, the Twins lay in wait beneath the fruit tree where Seven Macaw habitually came to feed. At length, when he appeared, they opened fire with their blowguns. Hunahpu scored a direct hit which dislocated the bird's jaw. Stunned by the surprise attack, Seven Macaw plummeted to Earth behind the tree.

But as Hunahpu rushed up to finish off his quarry, the bird seized his arm in its powerful beak and wrenched it from his shoulder. Hunahpu was left with a bleeding wound. The first engagement between Seven Macaw and the Hero Twins thus ended in stalemate. Evidently, an even greater effort was required to rid the world of the conceited monster.

In the next phase of the battle, the Hero Twins employed subterfuge in preference to direct assault. The scene opens with the slow progress home of Seven Macaw, who was carrying Hunahpu's arm and nursing his injured jaw. He told his wife about being ambushed by the Hero Twins: "They shot me with their blowguns and dislocated my jaw; now my teeth are all loose and I've got a terrible toothache." Yet despite being in excruciating pain, Seven Macaw hung Hunahpu's arm over his fire and dared the boys to come and retrieve it.

The Powers of Birds and Beasts

Animals and birds played a prominent role in Maya religion and myth. Certain species were identified with gods and celestial bodies, or were assigned social or calendrical significance.

The jaguar, revered as the top predator of the Maya rainforest, naturally came to be associated closely with the principal heavenly body, the sun. In addition, the Maya venerated a wide range of jaguar gods, variously identified with the Underworld, the night, caves, stealth and hunting.

Another clear association was that between the wrinkled reptilian caiman and the old supreme deity of the Maya, Itzamna. Less obvious was the widely perceived affinity between the rabbit and the moon; a rabbit's profile was thought to be visible in the full moon.

Animals and birds also had a major symbolic function in the naming of people, clans and days and years on the sacred Maya calendar. Two of the first four human beings were called Jaguar Quitze and Jaguar Night. The harpy eagle was the personification of both the 20-year *katun* and the 400-year *baktun* calendrical cycles. The divine twins One Monkey and One Artisan (see pages 42–43) together were used to signify the eleventh day (Chuen), of the Maya calendar, on which shamans divined the future. Children born on this day were thought happy and fortunate.

masquerading as travelling shamans who specialized in curing toothache. The elders pronounced themselves happy to take part in this charade, and so the four set off for Seven Macaw's house.

Seven Macaw's Defeat

The monster sat wracked with pain by the toothache that his jaw injury had caused. Nevertheless, when the elders arrived, he observed the custom of greeting them with elaborate courtesies. He then enquired after the identity of the old couple's "children", and was told that they were orphans who travelled around with them, living off their leftovers.

Satisfied with this answer, Seven Macaw then asked the elders what "poisons" they could cure. In a comically self-pitying speech, he gave vent to the agony that his teeth were putting him through. "It's unbearable," he moaned, "I can't sleep and my eyes are sore. My teeth are all loose and I can't eat anything. Take pity on me!" "Very well, your lordship," replied the elders, "our diagnosis is that a worm is eating your jaw bone." (Interestingly, the Quiché Maya still believe that toothache is caused by worms.) The elderly couple then told Seven Macaw that, in order to get the worm out, they would have to extract his teeth; this remedy would also, they claimed, cure his eyes.

Vain as he was, the bird was alarmed at the thought of losing his beautiful teeth, but the elders reassured him that they would replace them with false teeth in "ground bone" of the very finest quality. Seven Macaw was thus persuaded, and the bogus shamans set to work, removing the monster's teeth of exquisite blue gemstones. However,

Meanwhile the Hero Twins approached two venerable white-haired elders to help them retrieve Hunahpu's arm and finally vanquish the monster. The first elder was a grandfather called Great White Peccary, the second a grandmother by the name of Great White Coati. The twins contrived a deception that involved them posing as the elders' orphaned grandchildren. The two old people were to approach Seven Macaw

36

they did not substitute them with ground bone teeth as they had promised, but only with kernels of white corn, and then proceeded to strip the area around his eyes of its precious metal. While the elders went about their task, the bird felt no pain and suspected nothing.

The image of the bird's dislocated jaw in this myth is thought to allude to the peculiar shape of the beak of the real scarlet macaw, with its large upper mandible and smaller lower one. Similarly, the removal of the metal discs around Seven Macaw's eyes is believed to explain the origin of the featherless white patches around the eyes of the real scarlet macaw.

The supposed "cure" applied by the elders simply succeeded in robbing Seven Macaw of all the signs of his prestige. And since his status rested entirely on outward show, he was nothing once divested of his gold and jewels. He promptly wasted away before their very eyes.

The episode thus concludes with total victory for the Hero Twins and with great rewards being bestowed on their helpers. As well as inheriting the huge amounts of wealth that Seven Macaw had amassed, the elders (who really were gifted doctors when they wanted to be) even managed to fit Hunahpu's severed arm back into its socket and make it as good as new.

Seven Macaw in the Heavens

Despite his depiction as an absurd and foolish figure in this tale, Seven Macaw had profound mythological and astronomical significance for the Maya people. They associated him with the seven stars that comprise the constellation of the Plough or Big Dipper, the rising and falling of which mark the beginning and end of the hurricane season in Central America. So according to some scholars, Seven Macaw's fall from the tree after being hit by

Hunahpu's blowgun pellet represented the descent of the constellation during the month of July.

Furthermore, the sequence of events as described in the *Popol Vuh* had a particular symbolic resonance. Seven Macaw and his two sons came to prominence in the immediate aftermath of the terrible universal flood that Hurricane summoned up in order to sweep away the wooden people (see page 31). The Maya would probably have associated the onset of the torrential tropical rains that accompanied the rise of Ursa Major every year with this great mythological deluge.

The legend of Seven Macaw and his sons also had a clear didactic purpose, acting as a cautionary tale about the perils of overweening pride and personal vanity. Above all, the Maya valued modesty in their heroes; in common with many of the other characters in Maya mythology, it is the total absence of this quality in the monstrous bird and his offspring that seals their fate.

The ambush which leads to the final defeat of Seven Macaw is seen in this ceramic pot. In the foreground kneels the Hero Twin Hunahpu, who aims his blowgun at the bird deity.

Zipacna and Earthquake

Having destroyed Seven Macaw, the Hero Twins still had to deal with his sons Zipacna and Earthquake, who had inherited their father's insufferable arrogance. The elder son, Zipacna, called himself "the maker of mountains", while his brother Earthquake styled himself "breaker of mountains".

The Hero Twins' defeat of the offspring of Seven Macaw is prefaced by the story of an earlier attempt to destroy his first son, Zipacna. In this tale, a group of proto-humans called the Four Hundred Boys enlisted Zipacna's help in carrying a huge tree trunk, but became alarmed at his enormous strength. So, they plotted to murder him by dropping the tree on top of him as he dug a hole for them. But Zipacna realized what was afoot and, quickly excavating a side tunnel, scrambled into it in the nick of time. In order to convince the boys that he was dead, he then cut off pieces of his nails and tufts of his hair and gave them to ants to carry to the surface. By and by, when the boys had drunk themselves into a stupor in celebration, Zipacna burst out of the ground, collapsed the hut and killed them all. The boys ascended to Heaven and became the Pleiades.

The Hero Twins were deeply saddened at the loss of the Four Hundred Boys, and resolved to

One of the Hero Twins presents the head and body of Zipacna – packed neatly in a jar – to the Maya's major deity Itzamna on this roll-out of a Maya burial vessel.

kill Zipacna. Taking flowers and a large flagstone, they constructed a fake crab as a decoy to lure the gluttonous monster to his death. They placed it in a deep canyon, and told Zipacna about the juicy meal awaiting him. On reaching the canyon Zipacna let himself down to eat the crab. But the rock that made the false crustacean's back had been balanced in such a way that it rolled on top of him the instant he touched it. He struggled free, but immediately returned. At this point, the story leaves it unclear whether Zipacna fell headlong down the canyon and broke his neck, or choked to death on the "crab". In any event, the incident spelt the end of him; now it only remained for Hunahpu and Xbalanque to conquer Earthquake.

Earthquake's Downfall

Seven Macaw's second son, Earthquake, grew larger and heavier than even the sun. As this threatened to disrupt the divine order, the founder god Heart of Sky ordered the Hero Twins to end Earthquake's existence.

Like his gargantuan brother Zipacna, Earthquake spent his time roaming the world destroying things, including his brother's work. Thus, where Zipacna had raised a mountain, Earthquake would knock it flat.

Once again, Hunahpu and Xbalanque used guile to approach Earthquake. Passing themselves off as simple hunters, they excited his curiosity by telling him about a new mountain they had seen rising in the east. Earthquake told them to take him there, boasting that he would destroy it.

They set off in single file, with Earthquake walking between the two boys. On their journey, the Twins shot birds with their blowpipes. Their hunting prowess impressed their companion, as did their skilful preparation of the wildfowl. Before cooking the birds, the boys smeared them with plaster ground from rocks dug from the soil. What Earthquake did not realize, however, was that they were practising magic: in smothering the birds thus, the Twins were anticipating Earthquake's own enclosure in the soil after his death.

Earthquake ate greedily and they went on their way. But just as they arrived at the mountain, the monster's strength left him; the magic coating on the birds had taken effect. He instantly fell down dead. The Twins bound his wrists and ankles and buried him in the Earth. Thus the world was finally rid of the last of the monsters.

The Birth of the Hero Twins

The *Popol Vuh* interrupts its narrative of the adventures of the Hero Twins to recount their genesis and early life. Like their later exploits, this is a story of unrelenting conflict and turmoil. In particular, their campaign against misrule of the Earth must be seen in the light of the destruction of their father and uncle by the Lords of the Underworld.

The twin deities One Hunahpu and Seven Hunahpu – respectively the father and the uncle of the future Hero Twins – had one abiding passion: the ballgame. So noisy was one of their hard-fought contests that it drew the attention of the main lords of the Underworld realm of Xibalba, One Death and Seven Death. They resolved to summon the twins to attend them, kill them and annex their ballcourt. Accordingly, they dispatched four owls to lead One Hunahpu and Seven Hunahpu down into the bowels of the Earth. On their way down, the twins had to traverse deep canyons, cross rivers of blood and pus, cross barriers of spikes and fight armies of scorpions. They survived these hardships, and eventually arrived in Xibalba. Here, they were set three tests by the Underworld lords. First the lords dressed up manikins to look like themselves; when One Hunahpu and Seven Hunahpu greeted these counterfeits respectfully, the real lords laughed derisively. Then they fooled the twins into sitting on a hot stone. Finally, each twin was given a lighted torch and a cigar, with the instruction that they must be returned in the morning "just as they look now". On failing this final, unpassable test, they were executed and buried in the Underworld ballcourt.

Before interring the twins, the Underworld lords severed One Hunahpu's head, changed it into a gourd and placed it in the fork of a tree. The tree promptly bore a great crop of fruit, which no-one was allowed to touch. But a young woman, Blood Moon (Mayan: Xquic), daughter of the Lord Blood Gatherer, tried to pick the gourd that had once been One Hunahpu's skull. As she did so, the gods ordained that the gourd spat into her hand, making her pregnant with Hunahpu and Xbalanque. When Blood Gatherer learned of his daughter's indiscretion, he flew into a rage and ordered her sacrifice. But Blood Moon persuaded the messenger owls sent to conduct her to her execution to spare her. They deceived the Underworld lords with a lump of red cochineal resin in the shape of Blood Moon's heart. This ruse gained her enough time to reach the upper world.

The birth of the Hero Twins, whose mother Blood Moon was impregnated by a gourd, was a momentous event in the history of the Quiché. This terracotta figure of a pregnant woman is from the Guatemala highlands.

The Ballgame

The ballgame was played throughout Mesoamerica. The ball was made of solid rubber and the game usually took place in a masonry ballcourt. Although the exact rules are not known, some elements of the game have been reconstructed from artistic depictions, early Spanish accounts and archaeological evidence.

The Mesoamerican ballgame may have been somewhat akin to rugby or American football, the object being to get the ball into the endzones. At some courts, however, stone rings have been found on top of the side walls, suggesting that a player scored by hitting the ball through the rings.

Players were forbidden to use their hands or feet; instead, they hit the ball with their knees, elbows and hips. Depictions of the game show players wearing extensive padding on these parts of their bodies.

Ballcourts were generally shaped like a capital "I" and had either vertical or sloping side walls. Court sizes varied enormously; while some could accommodate only one or two players per side, others are on a grand scale (such as the court at Chichen Itza, which measures some 168 metres in length).

The ballgame was not just a focus of entertainment. In some cultures, it became a symbolic re-enactment of conflict, and incorporated ritual human sacrifice. Along the side walls of the court at Chichen Itza is a long stone frieze depicting the aftermath of a game. The captain of the defeated team kneels on the ground, his head severed, with streams of blood gushing from his neck. At the centre of the ball is a skull. This calls to mind the scene from the *Popol Vuh* where Xbalanque is forced to play the game using his brother's head. To the Maya, the ballgame would have been seen as a recreation of the battle between the Hero Twins and the Lords of the Underworld.

The ballgame is thought to have been played by the earliest Mesoamerican cultures, such as the Olmec. It was more than a sport; such was its importance that courts, like this one at Copán, were often built as part of ceremonial complexes.

Once there, Blood Moon sought out Xmucane, the mother of One Hunahpu and Seven Hunahpu. Xmucane set the girl an impossible task to test her credentials: she was told to bring home a whole netful of maize from just one plant. But as the gods wished to ensure the safe birth of the twins, they intervened to help Blood Moon, and so she was accepted by Xmucane.

Hunahpu and Xbalanque's Childhood

When the Hero Twins were growing up, their grandmother Xmucane spurned them. They also had to contend with the jealousy of their half-brothers – the twins One Monkey and One Artisan. The Hero Twins had to hunt for the entire family, but thrived on the outdoor life. By contrast, One Monkey and One Artisan stayed at home, currying Xmucane's favour with their musical and artistic skills. When the Hero Twins returned laden with game, Xmucane prepared food only for herself and the older boys, leaving the providers to live off leftovers.

At first the Hero Twins put up with this contemptuous treatment, but eventually they rebelled. Returning one day empty-handed, they reported that the birds they had shot had got entangled in a high tree. Their half-brothers foolishly agreed to come and help retrieve them. As they shinned up the tree, Hunahpu and Xbalanque made the trunk grow, leaving them stranded, and then called up to them: "Undo your loincloths and let the ends dangle behind you!" The brothers obeyed, and were instantly turned into forest monkeys. The only sounds these two great singers could now make were howls and shrieks. Even their grandmother, who was distraught when she heard what had happened, could not help laughing when she saw their absurd new guises.

The Twins later came upon their father and uncle's ball-game equipment and taught themselves how to play. Like One and Seven Hunahpu

This ceramic ballplayer wears a garment made from a full jaguar pelt draped around his waist, as protection against the rough stone surface of the court. His necklace is made, in part, from the skulls of beaten opponents.

42

One Monkey and One Artisan

One Monkey and One Artisan were the first set of twin sons of One Hunahpu, and had been present at the fateful ballgame when their father and uncle were led away to the Underworld. Unlike the unselfconscious "doers" Hunahpu and Xbalanque, the elder twins are portrayed in the Popol Vuh as reflective thinkers.

Skilled and industrious, One Monkey and One Artisan became the patron gods of art. This Classic period frieze is decorated with a row of dancing spider monkeys.

One Monkey and One Artisan are depicted as lazy "stay-at-homes", with an evil streak in their characters. They made two failed attempts on the lives of their infant half-brothers, the Hero Twins, by abandoning them on an anthill and in a bramble thicket. The elder twins' resentment only increased as they saw the Hero Twins grow up to become active, carefree adolescents.

Yet the elder twins also had positive traits. They were diligent, accomplished in many forms of art and gifted with prescience. They were venerated throughout Mesoamerica as the patron deities of all artists, musicians and dancers. The Aztecs believed that those lucky enough to be born under the day-sign One Monkey would become singers, dancers or scribes.

before them, they were summoned by the Lords of Xibalba, yet the Hero Twins proved more cunning and resourceful than their forebears. They circumvented the graven images by creating a mosquito which bit the real lords and made them cry out. Similarly, they won through the ordeal of the torches and cigars by extinguishing them and substituting red macaw feathers for the torch flames and fireflies for the glow of the cigars.

On subsequent nights, the Twins endured ordeals in the House of Knives, the House of Cold, the House of the Jaguars and the House of Fire. Their final sojourn was in the House of Zotz the Killer Bat. Throughout the night, they held the

bat at bay, but when Hunahpu peered out in the morning, he was decapitated and his head was carried off to the Xibalbans. Xbalanque then devised a plan to resurrect his brother. He first took a squash and carved it into a likeness of his brother's features. He and the headless Hunahpu then returned to the ballcourt for another match against the gods, only this time using Hunahpu's real head as a ball. During the game, Xbalanque deliberately hit his brother's head into the woods, where he switched it for the squash. When play resumed, the squash burst, and the tricked gods were defeated. Hunahpu's head was restored to his body and he was made whole again.

The Defeat of the Underworld Gods

The Hero Twins – Hunahpuh and Xbalanque – had to undergo a series of ordeals that the evil Lords of Xibalba devised for them. But they had learned from the mistakes of their forefathers. Every time, by their cunning, courage and perseverance, the Twins succeeded in outwitting the malevolent Underworld gods. Nevertheless, it was not enough for the Twins to survive: they had to win. To truly avenge the cruel deaths of their father and uncle, the Hero Twins had also to bring about the annihilation of the Lords One and Seven Death. In other words, they had to overcome death itself.

Underworld creatures take part in a macabre dance of death along the side of a cylindrical funerary vessel. The central figure has skull-like features and prances gleefully in front of a sacrificial altar. On the far right sits a dog, grinning because he has been brought back to life. Above him hovers the firefly that the Hero Twins used to light their cigars. Such comical images of Xibalba were common in Maya art.

The next test set for the Hero Twins by the Lords of Xibalba involved them having to leap over a pit of fire. Faced with this ordeal, the boys flung themselves straight into the flames. The gods thought that the Twins had perished, so they rejoiced and scattered their ashes in the river. But Hunahpu and Xbalanque's bodies were reconstituted in the water. Five days later they emerged in the form of half-fish, half-beautiful young men.

The Hero Twins then disguised themselves as ragged, itinerant performers and went back to Xibalba. At first they entertained the commoners, but news of their wonderful show soon reached One and Seven Death, who summoned them to perform in their palace. The Twins began their act

there with various animal dances, and went on to demonstrate a number of miracles. They burned down a house full of lords and restored it to new again without injuring a single person. They repeated this trick with a dog. But even these spectacular feats failed to satisfy the gods, who begged the Twins to provide them with bigger thrills. "Sacrifice someone without killing them!" they yelled. The twins accomplished this easily, and the gods, now whipped up into a frenzy, cried: "Do it to yourselves!" So, Xbalanque ripped out his brother's heart and revived him on the spot. "Now do the same for us!" demanded One and Seven Death. "But of course," replied the crafty twins suavely, "what is death to the gods?"

And so they killed One Death, the chief lord of Xibalba. At this, the other great lord, Seven Death, suddenly grew meek and begged for mercy. But Hunahpu and Xbalanque marched him and all the lesser lords to a canyon and hurled them to their deaths. Then the Twins revealed their true identities to the people of Xibalba, and invoked the names of their father and uncle. The terrified Xibalbans expected to be executed, but the Twins agreed to spare them on condition that they no longer demand human sacrifice.

The final act of the victorious brothers in the Underworld was to disinter the remains of One and Seven Hunahpu from the ballcourt. They reassured their forebears that future generations would honour their memories. After reporting that they had "cleared the road of death, loss and pain," they ascended to the upper world. Their duty done, the Hero Twins were taken up into the sky, where one of them became the sun and the other the moon, though Maya myth is unclear as to which brother becomes which celestial body.

Ceramics for the Dead

The Maya custom of burying food and precious objects, such as jade or obsidian carvings, for the dead in pottery containers provided a convenient medium for detailed depictions of the Underworld and its sometimes outlandish denizens.

On this Maya funerary vessel, the skeletal Lord of the Dead (*centre*) dances with his bizarre menagerie.

Some of the most spectacular Mesoamerican imagery of the Late and Postclassic periods is found on painted pottery left in Maya graves. Sites range from elaborate tombs in temples at Tikal or Copán to simple burials under the floors of houses.

From the island of Jaina off the Campeche coast, which may have been used as a necropolis, come elegant miniature figures depicting nobles and gods. Even more striking are polychrome pots painted in the so-called "codex style". The loose style sometimes calls to mind the free-flowing graphic invention of 20th-century comic-books.

The painters' subject-matter is often the Underworld, known to the Maya as Xibalba, the "Place of Fright". Some authorities have suggested that these scenes may have derived from a now-lost codex detailing the soul's journey through Xibalba after death rather in the manner of the Egyptian *Book of the Dead*. The treatment is often comical, reflecting the

Maya's ambivalent relationship with death – part fascination and part derision.

The sometimes hallucinatory nature of the imagery may have reflected genuine experiences of altered consciousness: one recurring motif shows participants receiving ritual enemas, possibly of an intoxicating liquor or the hallucinogen peyote, administered from a leather or rubber syringe-bag fitted with a hollow bone tube.

The First People

The final stage in the Maya legend of creation concerns the emergence of human beings. For their third, successful attempt at making people, the founder gods Hurricane and Gucumatz chose maize as their raw material.

After their first two abortive attempts at fashioning human beings, Hurricane and Gucumatz prepared carefully when they tried for a third time. Only when the human race emerged would the gods be properly honoured and the sun, moon and stars make their appearance.

To assist them in their endeavour, the creator gods solicited the help of some of the animals they had already put upon the Earth. Four species – the fox, the coyote, the parrot and the crow – were sent out to scout for a suitable location for this new act of creation. At length, they came upon a mountainous site called "Split Place" or "Bitter Water Place", where useful plants grew in abundance. Many delicious fruits were there for the harvesting, such as cacao (chocolate), custard apples and sweet plums. Most important of all, however, were white and yellow strains of maize, which would form people's staple diet. The animals gathered the maize and took it to Xmucane, the grandmother of the Hero Twins. She ground up the grain, and then mixed it with water with which she had washed her hands.

Then she passed the mixture on to Hurricane and Gucumatz. Out of this dough-like paste they moulded the first human beings. At first they were just four in number; these were the ancestral fore-fathers of the Quiché Maya lineages. Their names were Jaguar Quitze, Jaguar Night, Not Right Now and Dark Jaguar. These first humans were known as "mother-fathers", for in future ceremonials they came to represent both the male and female parents of all their descendants, a tradition which continues to this day.

The mother-fathers were highly satisfactory. Unlike their failed predecessors, they could express themselves lucidly and comprehend well. They were pleasing to the eye and worked vigorously. One especially remarkable attribute was their supernatural vision, which allowed them to observe everything on Earth and in the sky. They could even see inside rocks and mountains and far into the ocean depths. At first, their creators approved of their thirst for knowledge, and encouraged them to investigate their surroundings to the full; in return, the humans were grateful to their benefactors.

But gradually, humans' boundless curiosity and comprehension threatened to rival the creator gods' own omniscience, and they began to regard their creations with less indulgence. They decided to put a limit on people's abilities. So, as if breathing on a mirror, Hurricane clouded their sharp vision, making them able henceforth only to see things that were relatively close at hand. Having been firmly put in their place, people were sure to remain loyal and subservient to the gods.

Next the gods made four women as wives for the men. Their names were Red Sea Turtle, Prawn House, Water Hummingbird and Macaw House. These "ladies of rank" gave birth to the many tribes that made up the Quiché people. Even before the advent of the sun and the beginning of recorded history, these early people multiplied and flourished. Their skins were of many colours and they spoke a variety of languages. Yet what united them was their shared anticipation of the first sunrise. Without exception, they were devout believers who prayed fervently to their creators, beseeching them to safeguard their children's future. They humbly implored the gods to give them light and a safe place to live, and to ensure their prosperity and well-being. As well as paying homage to the gods of Heaven, the first people worshipped the divine hero One Hunahpu and his ancient mother Xmucane.

As they conducted their prayer and fasting, the first people kept a constant lookout to the east. They knew that the first sunrise would be preceded by the ascent of the planet Venus, and looked forward to the "dawning and sowing" that would confirm their place on Earth. When the sun finally did appear, life-giving heat would permeate throughout the Earth, and the people's lives would take on a new coherence and purpose. However, the first dawn was so long in coming that the people became downhearted. They wandered around aimlessly in the darkness, with no sense of belonging to a place and with no conception of social order.

Migrating ceaselessly across the land, they eventually settled at a place known as Tulan Zuyua ("Seven Caves, Seven Canyons"). At this site, they acquired their patron deities; the most important was the one-legged god Tohil. As a bringer of fire, Tohil was a great benefactor to the people, but he also demanded regular human sacrifice. His character soon became evident when a hail storm suddenly extinguished all the fires in Tulan Zuyua. The tribes were half-paralyzed with cold, so Tohil offered to restore the gift of fire to them by grinding his heel into his sandal. Yet this help came at a price; the people had to agree to the principle of humans being "suckled on their side" by the god. This meant that victims' hearts would be cut out through a hole in their ribcage. According to the Quiché, this was the origin of human sacrifice. Still yearning for the rise of Venus and the sun, the people soon began to migrate away from Tulan Zuyua towards the east. Dignified and resourceful though these early people were, they had no

Although this figurine of a Maya woman is thought to represent a courtesan, it displays the stateliness and dignity that this culture regarded as essential feminine virtues.

47

possessions and were dressed in animal skins. They endured great hardships; stumbling around in the darkness, they could find nothing to eat and were gradually becoming parched with thirst.

In the midst of this suffering, the "mother-fathers" climbed up a mountain called Place of Advice, and there resolved to turn the mass starvation into an act of penance. Tohil and the other gods were moved at this, and responded by ordering Jaguar Quitze and his companions to keep their sacred images safe. Accordingly, although they were exhausted by their long vigil, the forefathers searched high and low for secure places in which to conceal the images of the deities. For example, the effigy of the god Hacauitz was hidden on a mountain top, attended by his adherents as they waited for the first dawn. And suddenly, the dawn began. First the "sun carrier" Venus became visible above the horizon. In their happiness, Jaguar Quitze and his fellows "cried sweetly" and burned incense in gratitude. Then the sun itself came up. As it did so, all the birds and animals rose up from the valleys and lowlands and watched the joyous spectacle from the mountain tops. The birds spread their wings in the new warmth of the sun's rays and the first human beings knelt in prayer. However, so intense was the sun's power that the old gods were turned to stone, along with the first dangerous wild animals, the forerunners of the modern puma, jaguar, rattlesnake and fer-de-lance. Just one small god,

A new day dawns over the imposing site of Chichen Itza on the Yucatán peninsula. On the left stands a figure of a standard bearer, while on the right is the Pyramid of Kukulcan.

How the People of Corn Started Farming

The development of Mesoamerican culture from hunter-gatherer societies to great urban civilizations was founded on the cultivation of four crops – beans, squashes, chillis and maize. Of these, maize was of paramount importance.

An early cultivated form of maize was first grown in the Tehuacan valley in Puebla in central Mexico around 5000 years before the Spanish Conquest. Some 2000 years later, during the Formative period, hybridization of this crop with a related wild grass known as *teosinte* had produced larger, more productive strains. The domestication of maize was highly significant, since it formed the basis of settled arable farming in the region. As a result, the population of Central Mexico grew dramatically and began to congregate in large villages. Early peoples' diet of corn was supplemented with beans and chillis. Together with several varieties of squash and tomato, these provided essential vitamins and proteins.

The central role played by maize in the rise of Mesoamerican civilization is reflected in the mythology of the Maya. A variant of the myth of One Hunahpu in the *Popol Vuh*, who was decapitated by the Lords of Xibalba (see page 43), portrays him as the god of maize. His severed head is represented as a corn cob, whose seeds sprout and rise from the "Underworld" (i.e. below the Earth). In this account, then, the Hero Twins' descent into the Underworld to retrieve their father's remains clearly symbolizes the human quest for corn as the staple of life. Nor can it be a coincidence that this text describes the first human beings as having been created from maize (see pages 46–47).

Finally, there is an episode in the *Popol Vuh*, immediately preceding the defeat of the Underworld gods, which describes how the hunters Hunahpu and Xbalanque were charged with tending their grandmother Xmucane's garden. Wishing to avoid any exertion, they used magic to make their tools do their work for them. According to Mesoamerican scholars, this brief

This stone effigy of a maize god shows a human figure surrounded by the cobs of corn that formed the main food crop of all Mesoamerican societies.

interlude may symbolize the change from a society based purely on hunting to one reliant on a combination of game hunting and domesticated vegetables and grains.

Though maize was the main food crop throughout Mesoamerica, the Maya, who traced their origins to the "people of corn", had a particular affinity with it. Artefacts often depict corn cobs as human heads; conversely, the Maya are thought to have practised cranial deformation to mimic the elongated form of maize.

White Sparkstriker, fled into the shade and so avoided being petrified. The sun that rose at the first dawn is described in the *Popol Vuh* as being "like a person with a hot face". Its rays were so concentrated that the Earth's surface – which had been wet and muddy – dried out completely. However, gradually, as time passed, the power of the sun's rays lessened, making life on Earth more tolerable for all living beings.

When the tribal forefathers witnessed the first dawn, they performed a solemn act of remembrance for those who had not survived the arduous journey. They also gave thanks to the gods Tohil, Auilix and Hacauitz. Because they were poor, they mixed in scraps of resinous bark and marigolds with the refined copal incense burnt in this ritual. The spirit of Tohil then spoke through his stone image and commanded the people to make sacrifices of deer and birds to the gods. So, on their hunting expeditions, although the people killed many deer and birds, they ate only the larvae of hornets, bees and wasps. When they returned home, they poured the blood of these mammals and birds into the mouths of their gods' effigies. At this time, the people of the "motherfathers" avoided others and lived secretly in the forest. Whenever other groups passed by, they concealed their whereabouts by imitating the calls of birds and animals. Presently, however, their patron gods became

dissatisfied over the question of sacrificial offerings. They reminded their chosen people of the pledge they had made to perform human sacrifice. To meet their obligations, therefore, the ancestors of the Quiché began to ambush small groups of hunters from other tribal groups. They cut open their victims' sides, offering up their hearts and blood to the gods.

At first, the tribespeople whose members had been waylaid and ritually slaughtered thought that wild animals were responsible for their disappearance. But when the truth dawned on them, they determined to capture the images of the gods for themselves. They tried first to track down the worshippers of Tohil, Auilix and Hacauitz, but the Quichés' ancestors were too clever for them. However, they did come across the spirits of the gods, who had taken on the guise of three handsome youths bathing in the river. The tribespeople devised a plan to trap the boys, by sending three lovely young women down to the river to seduce them. But the spirits of the gods realized immediately that this was a trick and, spurning the lovely girls' advances, sent them straight back to the tribal chiefs with a gift of three cloaks, exquisitely embroidered with motifs of a jaguar, an eagle and hornets. The tribal chiefs were delighted with the fine cloaks and put them on, whereupon the embroidered creatures came

A seated man prepares for a bloodletting rite. The *Popol Vuh* traces the origin of auto-sacrifice to the earliest days of the Maya.

This roll-out image of a vase shows lords resplendent in their ceremonial regalia. The figure on the far right is wearing a hornet-covered cloak like the one given to the tribal chief in the *Popol Vuh.*

to life and attacked them. The angry tribesmen were humiliated by having fallen for this ruse, and prepared to make war on their enemies.

In the great conflict that ensued, the tribespeople gathered for an assault on the capital of the Quichés' ancestors. They donned their full battle regalia and marched on the city. However, on the way, the army was entranced and fell into a deep sleep. The defenders stole up on the sleeping tribespeople and humiliated them again by plucking out their beards and eyebrows and stealing their war trophies. Then the Quiché returned to their citadel where they set up wooden manikins along the ramparts. Tohil advised them to collect wasps and hornets, and fill four big gourds with them. When the attackers finally arrived in full cry, they were deceived by manikins moving on top of the citadel walls. Then suddenly the defenders unleashed the contents of the gourds on the tribespeople. Agonisingly stung on their arms and faces, they were in no fit state to resist when the Quichés' ancestors emerged from the city and cut them down with bows and axes. The survivors were spared on condition that the tribespeople pay tribute in perpetuity.

This triumphal episode of Quiché mythic history ends with the death of the ancestral forefathers. When they realized death was approaching, the forefathers began to sing a lament. They announced that the "time of our Lord Deer" had come, namely that the current solar year would soon be replaced by one beginning with the day named after the Deer. They explained that their work was complete and that the time had come for them to return to their place of origin.

Jaguar Quitze then bestowed on his people a sacred object called the "Bundle of Flames"; this carefully secured artefact would, he explained, represent his continuing presence and power among them after his death. Then the ancestors vanished, never to be seen again. A holy day was instituted in remembrance of the "mother-fathers" – the Day of the Lord Deer, which also became known as the Day of the Sacred Bundle.

The Quiché People

The first men, Jaguar Quitze and his brothers, had three sons – Noble Two, Noble Acutec and Noble Lord. These founders of the major Quiché patrilineal families embarked on a pilgrimage to the east to seek the place of their fathers' origin.

As the leaders of the tribe, the three nobles realized that their skills and wisdom would be missed while they were away, and so reassured their people that they would return. Not long after they set out, they were received by a monarch in the Yucatán called Nacxit, who conferred on them the collective titles Keeper of the Mat and Keeper of the Reception House Mat. The first title is thought to refer to council leadership, and the second to tribute or tax collection.

Nacxit also gave the lords various emblems that would enhance their power when they returned home. According to the *Popol Vuh,* these were: "canopy and throne, bone flute and bird whistle, sparkling powder and yellow ochre [used as cosmetics], puma's paw and jaguar paw, head and hoof of deer, leather armband and snailshell rattle, tobacco gourd and food bowl, and finally parrot feathers and egret feathers."

Farther east, the lords were given manuscripts. This episode probably alludes to the original hieroglyphic *Popol Vuh,* for the eastern

Most of the buildings of the Quiché have been reduced to rubble. But Maya sites elsewhere give some idea of what the architecture must have been like. This magnificent palace in Northern Yucatán was built by the Puuc Maya in the ninth century. It is adorned with masks of the rain god Chac.

Yucatán was an important centre for the production of Maya codices. Returning to their citadel of Hacauitz, the nobles proudly displayed their new symbols. Their power had grown considerably, and they resumed their dominion over their own people and all the neighbouring tribes.

After the lords' journey to find their roots, further migrations ensued, and saw the founding of successive citadels, named "Thorny Place", "Bearded Place" and "Rotten Cane". Of these, Bearded Place was the greatest settlement. Here the Quiché were at peace, and civic life flourished. Their civilization was hallmarked by magnificent splendour, tempered with modesty; there was no foolishness, envy, arrogance or quarrelling in the city until a tribe called the Ilocs rebelled; they were roundly defeated and punished by being enslaved or sacrificed.

By the time Rotten Cane was founded, five generations had passed since the advent of light. Apart from its physical security on a rocky outcrop, Rotten Cane (or Quiché, as the town came

Pedro de Alvarado, the Spanish conquistador, subdues the Maya. Alvarado arrived in Mexico with Cortés and then struck out on his own to conquer lands to the south. His savage reputation is recorded in the *Popol Vuh.*

to be called) was renowned for the devout nature of its inhabitants. Its lords engaged in long penances and partial fasts which could last for up to a whole solar year. During these devotional activities, they would refrain from sexual activity and observe strict dietary restrictions. One important result of these austerities was a return of the clear vision and foresight that the first people had enjoyed before the gods clouded their vision (see page 47). The shaman lords also addressed the gods in a series of elaborate songs, praising Heart of Sky for the gifts of life and prosperity, and praying for continuing good fortune.

At the time that the *Popol Vuh* was written, eleven generations of lords had ruled peacefully over the Quiché Maya. Then, in the twelfth generation, during the rule of Three Deer and Nine Dog, a new name suddenly appears in the manuscript – Tonatiuh. This appellation, which means "he who travels getting hot", was given by the Nahuatl speakers of Mexico to Pedro de Alvarado, the notorious Spanish conqueror of Guatemala. Having begun by recounting the creation of human beings, the authors of the sacred text ended their mythical history poignantly with the destruction of their nation. "That is enough about the being of Quiché," the text concludes, "since it is no longer to be seen."

BONAMPAK

In 1946, an American photographer named Giles Healey, searching for Maya remains in the Mexican state of Chiapas, received exciting news. Local Indians told him of a previously unrevealed site deep in the rainforest. Guided by them, he discovered a three-chambered building containing a unique sequence of artworks that led his discovery to become known as Bonampak – "Painted Walls". Scholars have since copied and digitally enhanced the designs, restoring the original vivid colours. The result is a unique glimpse of Maya court life in the late 8th century AD, when the Classic era was approaching its end.

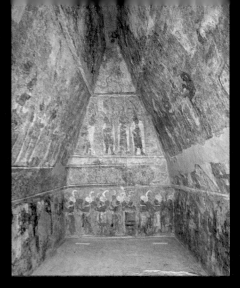

Above: Paintings crowd the walls and ceiling in the first of Bonampak's three rooms. The Maya used mineral and vegetable pigments on the stucco walls to produce these vivid colours.

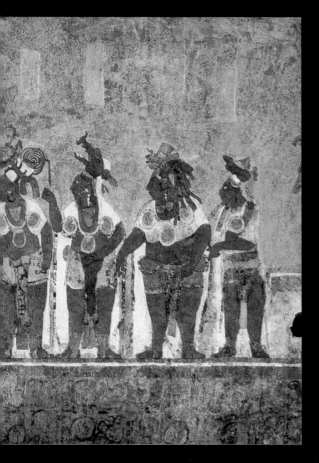

Left: Maya lords celebrate the accession of the heir to Bonampak. The painting is unfinished: each lord's name should have been written in the pale blue plaque above his head.

Left: Cleared of the vegetation that cloaked it until recent times, the ruins of Bonampak rise against a jungle backdrop.

Right: As musicians signal the start of the ceremony with sonorous trumpet blasts, fantastically-garbed figures portraying river gods act out a ritual whose significance is long forgotten. Glyphs at the site date the festivities to AD790 or 791.

A warlord takes a captive (*above*) in a detail from the battle scene that dominates Bonampak's second room. The final chamber (*left*) shows the conflict's aftermath; while the prisoners await their fate, the victor gives thanks to the gods by drawing blood from his tongue in an act of auto-sacrifice.

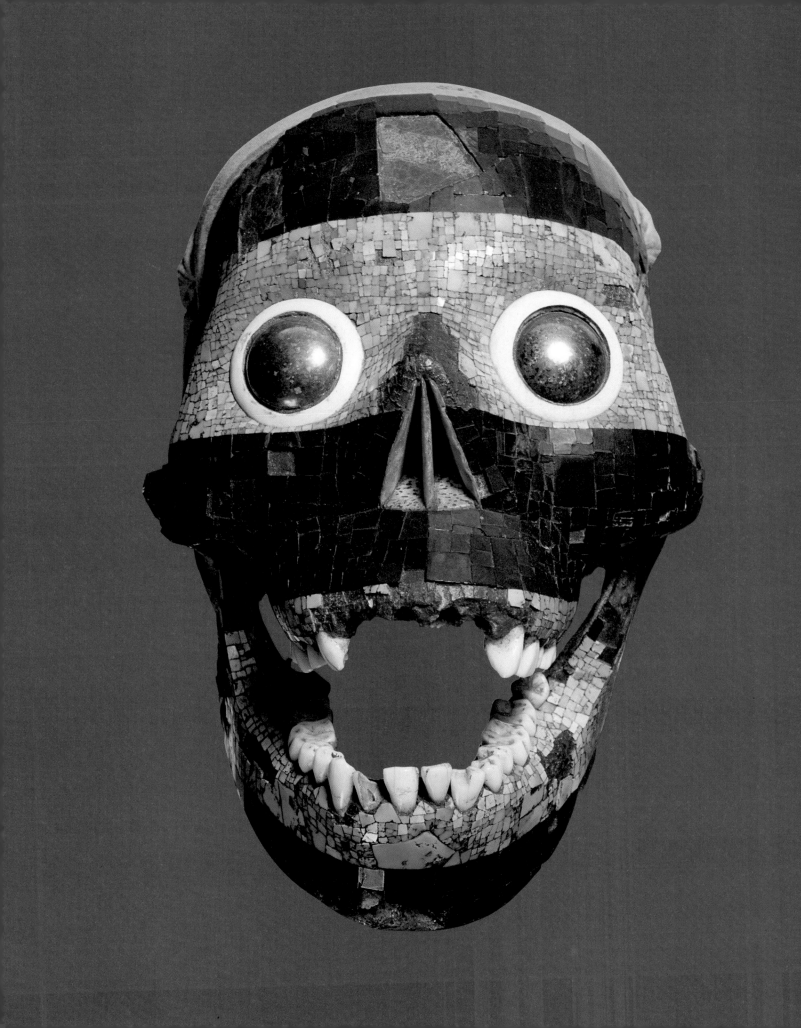

RAISING THE SKY

Because the Aztecs were the dominant group in Central America when the Spanish arrived, most of what we know about Mesoamerican myth comes from them. But as relative newcomers to the empire, they sought legitimacy by borrowing their gods from the succession of civilizations that had held sway in the Valley of Mexico for a thousand years before them. Their myths were, for the most part, the shared myths of the region.

The crowded Aztec pantheon of 1500 deities – which included Coatlicue, the Earth Mother and Tonatiuh the Sun God, as well as Tezcatlipoca the Dark Lord of Strife and his life-giving brother, Quetzalcoatl the Plumed Serpent – was believed to have intervened decisively in past human history. The only way the Aztecs could guarantee the continued support of these gods was by the offering of human sacrifice.

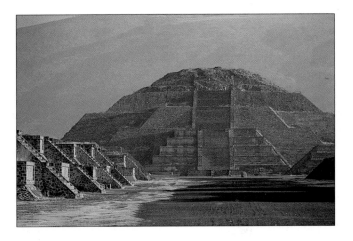

This bloody ritual arose from a fear of universal destruction. Different deities had already created four successive worlds, or "Suns", and each world had in turn been annihilated. By flood, wind, fire and devouring animals, the Earth and its people had perished, together with the gods themselves and even the mighty sun.

Ometeotl had created new gods to regenerate a new world: the Fifth Sun, which is the present age. These gods raised up the sky – which had collapsed on to the Earth – recreated the human race from the bones of its ancestors, and put the sun back in the heavens. But they also ordained that the Fifth Sun was to be the last: if it too were destroyed, there would be no more worlds. The price that the gods demanded for staving off this ultimate catastrophe was the blood and hearts of sacrificial victims.

The world came to know the elaborate edifice of Aztec myth largely from the pages of the *Florentine Codex* (named after the city where it is now kept) compiled by the Franciscan friar Bernardino de Sahagún. He came to Mexico in 1529 and spent twenty-five years on his great project: elderly Aztecs were questioned about the old days, their replies were recorded by specially trained scribes, and de Sahagún himself edited the results into a vast encyclopedia of Aztec life and thought.

Above: **The Pyramid of the Moon at Teotihuacan was built in the late Classic period and regarded with awe by people who came later.**

Opposite: **This human skull was inlaid with lignite, turquoise and shell and its eyes with pyrites to represent Tezcatlipoca, Dark Lord of Strife. It was attached by long leather straps to the back.**

57

An Unstable Universe

The Aztec cosmos had three layers. Above the Earth rose the thirteen levels of the heavens, at the top of which dwelled the creator Ometeotl. In the middle lay the Earth; and below this were the nine levels of Mictlan, the Underworld. But despite this apparently stable structure, the Aztecs believed that life on Earth was in daily peril.

As elsewhere in Mesoamerica, the Aztec cosmos was believed to have four directions emanating from a fixed centre. The directions were the cardinal points of north, south, east and west, whose meridians quartered the Earth. Many cultures believed that a tree grew in the centre of the world, rising up through layers of Heaven and sending roots down to the Underworld, but for the Aztecs the centre was their capital city of Tenochtitlan built on an island in the middle of the great Lake Texcoco.

This horizontal concept of the universe had its vertical counterpart. The world inhabited by human beings was a huge flat space, surrounded by the sea, and at a certain point, the sea curved up to become the sky; the upper air consisted of "sky waters" which might at any time fall and obliterate the Earth. This had in fact happened in one of the four mythological catastrophes that had anni-

The Two Lord, Ometeotl, was both man and woman. This Aztec stone sculpture shows him/her as master of fate with the mask of the star dragon on his headdress.

hilated the world (see pages 60–63). Such disasters were typical of the Aztec cosmos, which though unstable was nevertheless capable of regeneration.

How the World Was Made

Ometeotl, the supreme being, existed beyond time and space. As was common with Aztec mythological beings, Ometeotl had a dual nature, being at the same time both male and female, as signified by his/her alternative title of Lord of Duality. He/she dwelt in the highest of the thirteen heavens in a paradise known as the Place of Duality. The two-sexed god was also known as two separate deities Tonacatecuhtli and Tonacacihuatl, meaning "Lord of Our Sustenance" and "Lady of Our Sustenance", who were locked in coition. This mysterious concept of duality within unity was recurrent in Aztec cosmology. Ometeotl was the parent and source of all creation, and as Tonacatecuhtli is said to have brought the Earth to life with his breath. In the words of the Aztecs, the universe lay like a drop of water in the creator's hand, and people lay like a grain of seed within that droplet.

Thirteen Layers of the Sky

The Aztec Heaven extended upward from the Earth's surface in thirteen hemispheres, the uppermost of which was called Omeyocan, where the supreme being Ometeotl lived, eternally creating, organizing and sustaining the world with his/her holy breath.

At the centre of Tenochtitlan lay the Great Temple, as shown on this 16th-century Spanish map.

Below the Earth's surface lay Mictlan, the Underworld, which was created by Omeyocan's sons. The three levels of the cosmos – the heavens, the Underworld and the Earth's surface – converged at the centre of the world, the Aztec capital city of Tenochtitlan.

"Who would conquer Tenochtitlan? Who could shake the foundation of Heaven?" one Aztec poet cried, as if to say that were Tenochtitlan to be captured or destroyed, the universe itself would collapse. At the sacred centre of the sacred city stood the double temple of Huitzilopochtli (see pages 102–105), the Aztec national god, and the ancient god of rain, Tlaloc.

Ometeotl created the gods, but there his and her work ceased and all further creative activity was carried out by the other deities. Ometeotl was not, however, so ineffable and awe-inspiring that he/she could not be given a visual identity in Aztec sacred art. To emphasise the deity's primordial status, he/she was portrayed as an ancient being with a sagging jaw. The female half of Ometeotl was also associated with fire and the Pole Star. This connection with fire further associated the female Ometeotl with the fire goddess Chantico, who was herself the consort of the fire god Xiuhtecuhtli. Fire, which for the Aztecs included the pole of Heaven, thus provided Ometeotl's connection with the Pole Star.

Tonacatecuhtli and Tonacacihuatl ordained further creation through their four sons, whose number corresponded with the four sacred quarters of the Earth. At the same time as being separate deities, these sons were all aspects of an omnipresent god. The oldest was Red Tezcatlipoca or Xipe Totec, god of agriculture (see pages 90–91). The second and strongest was Black Tezcatlipoca, who later became known simply as Tezcatlipoca (see pages 70–73). The third was White Tezcatlipoca or Quetzalcoatl (see pages 74–75). The youngest and smallest was Huitzilopochtli, the warrior god who protected the Aztec nation (see pages 102–105), sometimes identified as Blue Tezcatlipoca.

These brothers helped create the world, the calendars, fire, the first man and woman, Oxomoco and Cipactonal, and the gods of rain and water (see pages 86–91).

The Five Suns

In four past ages, called "Suns", the world was destroyed when the sun itself was thrown out of the sky. Each age was presided over by a different god, who later destroyed it in an appropriate manner. For example, the goddess of water destroyed the Fourth Sun by flood, causing the heavens to fall down. The Fifth Sun was created when Ometeotl's four sons raised the sky.

The sun was commonly used as a decorative motif. In this gold pendant, dating from the Aztec period, it is represented as the bulbous god Tonatiuh.

The "Fifth Sun" was the age of the present, and the Aztecs performed constant rituals to ensure that the cosmic balance was maintained, for the world was a precarious place; one false move and it could tilt into chaos. Previous eras had been destroyed, and the next age always began when one of the other gods became the sun.

The four ages already past were named after the years in which they had ended. The first, for example, came to a close in the year Four Jaguar, and so the entire age took that name. Each of the four past ages was also associated with one of the elements of earth, air, fire and water. Likewise, each world age was identified with one of the five directions of the cosmos. Different peoples lived in each era and at its destruction, they were either killed or transformed. The Aztecs were very particular about the diets of each people, all of whom, until the present Sun, lived on seeds.

The First Sun

The first age was associated with the element of earth and was ruled over by Black Tezcatlipoca, the most powerful of the sons of Tonacatecuhtli and Tonacacihuatl. One day Tezcatlipoca decided to turn himself into the sun. During this "Sun of Earth", the world was populated by a race of giants, so large and strong that they could rip trees from the ground if they felt like it. They were vegetarians, living on a diet of pine nuts.

But the Sun of Earth ended exactly 676 years after it had been created. Quetzalcoatl, jealous of his brother shining so brightly in the sky, took his staff and struck Tezcatlipoca into the waters that surrounded the Earth. Then Tezcatlipoca turned into an enormous jaguar and devoured the entire race of giants. Later, he rose into the sky in the form of a mighty jaguar and became the constellation Ursa Major. Appropriately, this world met its end on the day Four Jaguar so it is also known as the Jaguar Sun.

The Suns of Wind, Rain and Water

The second world was created and ruled by Quetzalcoatl in his guise as the wind god Ehecatl. During this age, the "Sun of Wind", people evolved a little beyond the rudimentary habits of the giants, but they still lived simply on the seeds of the mesquite tree.

This time it was Tezcatlipoca's turn to strike down his rival Quetzalcoatl. All the people and their deity with them were carried away by a vast, dark hurricane that swept down on the Earth and blew them into the forest. The survivors of the wind were transformed into monkeys, the very ones – according to the legend – you can still see in the jungles of Central America today. This occurred in the year Four Wind, which gave its name to the era.

The third world, the "Sun of Rain", was presided over by Tlaloc, the god of rain and consequently also of fertility. This time, the human race discovered agriculture and began to cultivate a primitive form of grain. This world ended in the year Four Rain, when Quetzalcoatl created a rain of fiery ash, and the survivors were all transformed into butterflies, dogs and turkeys.

Chalchiuhtlicue or "She of the Jade Skirt" was the creator of the fourth world, the "Sun of Water". The wife of Tlaloc, she was the deity of running and still water: the oceans, rivers, lakes and streams. In this age the people of Earth subsisted on a seed called *acicintli*. The fourth world was destroyed when Chalchiuhtlicue made the waters under the Earth rush to the surface, causing a great flood. At the same time the sky collapsed and people were transformed into fish. This happened in the year Four Water.

The Fifth Sun

The present age is the Fifth Sun, known as Four Movement, created when the god Nanahuatzin sacrificed himself at Teotihuacan (see pages 84–85). Presided over by the fiery sun god Tonatiuh, whose name means "he who goes forth

The fertility goddess Chalchiuhtlicue, shown in this Aztec codex suckling a child, presided over the Fourth Sun.

Inic. v. parapho ypan mitoa inque
nin mochichivaya Ypepeyaca teteu.

(3) Tezcatlipuca.

paynal. (2)

vitzilopuchtli. (1)

quetzalcoatl. (4)

chicomecoatl (7)

chachalmeca (10)

totochtin. (5)

otontecuhtli (8)

yxcocauhqui (11)

tlalloc. (6)

yacatecutli (9)

ixtlilto. (12)

How Life Was Created After the Fourth Sun

The Aztecs believed that they were living in the Age of the Fifth Sun, which would end with a huge earthquake in the year Four Motion. Although no single source encompassed the way in which life had been recreated after the destruction of the preceding fourth world, a number of different myths described successive stages of the process.

The Fourth Sun was destroyed in an apocalyptic cataclysm in which the waters under the Earth rose to drown the world at the same time that the sky collapsed in upon it. Everything was drowned and washed away. Afterwards chaos reigned until Ometeotl's four sons, the chief gods of the Mesoamerican pantheon, transformed themselves into trees to lift up the firmament, thereby creating a space in which creation could once more begin. Another version of essentially the same story had the brother gods, Tezcatlipoca and Quetzalcoatl, making the sky and the Earth out of the torn body of the Earth monster Tlaltecuhtli (see page 107).

A separate myth told how Quetzalcoatl was also responsible for restoring humans to the Earth. To do so, he had to travel to the Underworld in search of all that was left of the fish people, their predecessors of the Fourth Sun: some bone in the possession of the sly and possessive Mictlantecuhtli, the skull-faced Central Mexican death god. Succeeding in his quest, Quetzalcoatl took the trophies to a mythical spot called Tamoanchan, literally "Land of the Misty Sky" (see pages 66–67). There, Quetzalcoatl's fellow gods decided to co-operate, and ground the bones up like maize and moistened the bone flour with their own blood. Then they fashioned people from the sticky dough. In Tamoanchan, the gods nurtured the infant humans until they were big enough to be sent down to the surface of the Earth by themselves.

A variant account had humans emerging fully formed from the bowels of the Earth. The place of origin was Chicomoztoc, "Seven Caves", a legendary mountain in whose womb-like inner recesses the human race was thought to have been miraculously generated.

This myth was particularly cherished by the nomadic Chichimec peoples of northern Mexico, many of whom traced their own tribal origins to Chicomoztoc. Among them were the Aztecs themselves, who included an account of a stopover there in the epic tale of the long trek that took them to the Valley of Mexico (see pages 96–99).

shining", it is the age of a fully evolved culture when the human race – and according to the myth the first people in this age were the inhabitants of Teotihuacan – at last cultivates maize, the Mesoamerican staple.

Bernardino de Sahagún included a visual guide to the gods in his work describing Aztec mythology, the *Florentine Codex*, which was written around 1570. In this detail, it is possible to pick out Tlaloc, Tezcatlipoca and Quetzalcoatl among others.

But war and disease also make their appearance during the Fifth Sun, and the world will eventually be consumed by earthquakes. After the earthquakes, time will come to an end forever. This event is inescapable, but can be postponed by satisfying the gods through the performance of ritual human sacrifices. All this, as Bernardino de Sahagún recorded in the *Florentine Codex*, will come to pass "when the Earth has become tired, when already it is all, when already it is so, when the seed of Earth has ended."

The Earth Mother

The Aztec Earth goddess was both horrifying and bountiful, hideous and radiant. In her character as the Earth itself she produced everything human beings needed to survive. In her celestial aspect she was the Milky Way, mother of the gods.

The Earth Mother was one of the oldest Aztec deities, known under several names and forms. As the Earth goddess, from whose body grew the essentials of the Aztec diet, she was known as Tonantzin, "Our Holy Mother", or Teteo Innan, "Mother of the Gods". But she was less an active god with a history of deeds than an ancient spiritual presence: someone who had always been there, dwelling within the Earth from the very beginning of time.

In another incarnation she was Toci, "Our Grandmother", a healing presence who was worshipped alongside Chicomecoatl in the annual harvest festival as the personification of nature's benevolence. Yet another avatar was as Yohualticitl, "Midwife of the Night". This healing divine presence presided over sweatbaths, which in the Aztec world were small, womb-like struc-

tures heated by fires built against their outside walls. People in need of physical or spiritual purification would crawl inside and sprinkle water on hot stones with a brush of scented herbs, filling the interior with fragrant steam. Then, after they had recited the prescribed hymns and prayers required by tradition, they would dash out to immerse themselves in cold water, cleansed both in body and in spirit.

The most obviously appealing of all the fertility goddesses was Xochiquetzal (see page 67), the epitome of feminine beauty and grace. A Venus figure who was sometimes said to be the lover of Quetzalcoatl, she was associated with the arts and

The goddess Tlazolteotl, "Eater of Filth", squats and unceremoniously defecates. Her association with sensuality and voluptuousness casts some light on the Aztec view of sex.

all forms of pleasure. A goddess of the Earth's abundance, she was also reputedly the first mother of twins and retained a lingering association with pregnancy and childbirth.

So too did a very different figure, the fearsome Tlazolteotl, who was often portrayed in the squatting position Aztec mothers generally adopted to give birth. As the filth Goddess, she was similarly associated with excrement and with the sexual lust of which it was the symbol. One of the nastier Aztec customs took place in her name. Young girls might be forced into prostitution in the

barracks for trainee warriors, only to be ceremonially killed once their career had reached an end, their bodies dumped as polluted refuse in the marshes of Lake Texcoco. Yet curiously this sinister, witch-like figure, identified with venereal diseases and the punishment of sexual excess, could absolve sin as well as inspire it.

The gap between the lovely and gracious flower goddess Xochiquetzal and the hag Tlazolteotl could hardly have been greater, but both represented aspects of the Aztec attitude to sexuality and the role of women in society.

Mistress of the Cycle of Birth and Death

The Mesoamerican people were natural accumulators who were always ready to expand the ranks of the gods. Coatlicue was a late incarnation of the Earth Mother worshipped by the Aztecs.

Coatlicue symbolized fecundity in her role as mother of the fire god Huitzilopochtli (see page 100), of the moon goddess Coyolxauhqui, and of the stars, her innumerable sons. But despite her fertility, she was also considered virginal by the Aztecs, who believed that Huitzilopochtli's conception was immaculate. This led certain Catholic commentators to associate this aspect of Coatlicue with the Virgin Mary.

But the goddess had a darker side to her. She was also associated with death and regeneration. Few representations of her survive, but in this aspect she is fearsome.

Coatlicue is the subject of one of the most celebrated of all Mexican sculptures – a giant statue of the goddess excavated in 1790 next to the cathedral in Mexico City. A pair of snakes are where her head should be; she wears a necklace of human hands, hearts and a skull; and her skirt is made of rattlesnakes. Her feet are a pair of giant claws.

Home of the Gods

The Aztec idea of paradise was in some ways close to the Garden of Eden. Tamoanchan was a beautiful place dominated by the World Tree which blossomed and bore fruit eternally. In most stories, its mistress was the goddess, Xochiquetzal, "Precious Flower".

Quetzalcoatl and Xolotl went to Tamoanchan when they returned from the Underworld with the bones of man's ancestors so that the Earth could be repopulated for its final age (see page 129). There they nourished the baby humans before sending them to live in the real world. As was the case with the Garden of Eden, the human race would never again return to this paradise. But Tamoanchan remained, though solely as a place for the gods to enjoy an idyllic existence away from the hurly-burly of human affairs and the violent activities of the other gods. In Tamoanchan, the deities feasted in perpetual summer on sacred maize, and had every other good thing to eat and

The Lord of Sustenance and his wife, who lived in paradise all the time, hunker over a bowl of blossoms in this detail from the *Codex Vaticanus.*

drink. At once a part of and remote from the world, it was said to be situated in the far south of Mexico on a mountain whose summit was almost as high as the moon.

Another account states that Tamoanchan was not on the Earth at all, but in the thirteenth and highest sphere of Heaven, where dwelled the supreme being Ometeotl – manifested as Tonacatecuhtli and Tonacacihuatl, the Lord and Lady of Our Sustenance. This Tamoanchan was the birthplace of the gods.

But even paradise could be touched by the turmoil and treachery of the gods, as two myths about Xochiquetzal show. This goddess of love was usually a beautiful maiden sometimes called the Virgin. But when she represented fruitfulness she was seen as a matron and identified with the Earth Mother herself (see pages 64–65). Xochiquetzal spent her time in Tamoanchan surrounded by her handmaidens, entertained by clowns and performing dwarves, and weaving the most delicate and exquisite textiles. Her gift to humanity was flowers, which were created from her vulva.

The World Tree was rooted in the Earth and passed through all the layers of Heaven before reaching the garden paradise of Tamoanchan. At each layer, its blossoms filled the air with scent.

Xochiquetzal's Love Life

As a matron Xochiquetzal was married to various gods. In one story, she was married to Tlaloc, but Tezcatlipoca – who was a serial seducer – wanted her for his own, so he carried her off to the Underworld where he raped her. Many scholars believe this story had a similar purpose to the Greek tale of Persephone's marriage to the Underworld lord Hades. Xochiquetzal's descent could be an attempt to explain the changing seasons or the death and rebirth of flowers.

The other myth associated with Xochiquetzal bears a curious resemblance to the Biblical story of the Fall, yet in this case instead of humans, it is an immortal who errs. In the midst of Tamoanchan grew a flowering tree whose everlasting leaves and flowers were filled with bird song. Although the gods were allowed every freedom in their home, the Lord of Sustenance forbade them to injure the tree. Xochiquetzal, however, tasted the fruit of the tree. The tree shook and fell asunder; it began to bleed as if wounded, so everyone knew of Xochiquetzal's transgression.

Like Eve, Xochiquetzal was the first woman to sin and her consumption of the forbidden fruit can be compared to sexual knowledge. Furious at her disobedience, the Lord of Sustenance cast Xochiquetzal out from Tamoanchan. On Earth, she became Ashen Eyes, Ixnextli, the goddess blinded by weeping. However in another version of the myth, it is all the gods who disobey the Lord of Sustenance, so they are all cast out of paradise to live in other layers of the universe. For this single mistake they are condemned to spend eternity bickering and fighting with each other.

Pulque, the Divine Intoxicant

Pulque was an alcoholic drink which the Aztecs made from the fermented sap of the maguey cactus and often used in rituals. How it came to be made available on Earth is the subject of one of the Aztec's most colourful myths.

The goddess Mayahuel wears a headdress decorated with green feathers, paper and rubber in this Aztec codex.

The magnificent maguey cactus that grows so abundantly in Mesoamerica had many important uses in Aztec society. The leaves served as roofing material and produced fibre for weaving. Leaves and roots, rich in vitamins A and B, contributed to at least thirty different foods and drinks, the most ritually significant of which was the intoxicating beverage pulque (or *octli*).

A vivid myth involving Quetzalcoatl and the beautiful young goddess Mayahuel explains the origin of pulque. When the gods observed the early humans, they saw that they never danced or sang, so the Plumed Serpent deity Quetzalcoatl decided that a stimulating drink like pulque would make them happier. Travelling to the heavens, Quetzalcoatl found the lovely Mayahuel, the granddaughter of one of the *tzitzimime*, a group of malevolent goddesses or star demons (see page 108), and persuaded her to come down with him to Earth.

When they reached Earth, the two gods entwined, transforming themselves into a single gigantic tree. Mayahuel was one fork and Quetzalcoatl the other. When the grandmother *tzitzimitl* discovered that Mayahuel was missing, she was utterly enraged. She summoned the star demons and together they swooped down to Earth in pursuit of the errant granddaughter.

As the *tzitzimime* arrived on Earth, the tree composed of Mayahuel and Quetzalcoatl split in two. Recognizing Mayahuel in one of its great branches, the grandmother *tzitzimitl* ripped the offending bough to pieces and fed it bit by bit to the other *tzitzimime*. Sorrowfully, Quetzalcoatl buried what was left of the beautiful Mayahuel's fleshless bones, and from these sprang the original maguey cactus that would later produce the joyfully intoxicating drink pulque.

Pulque was also associated with another group of deities known as the 400 Rabbits, for it was a rabbit that had discovered pulque when it nibbled the maguey plant. Images of these 400 rabbits were discovered buried at the base of the Great Temple at Tenochtitlan, leading some scholars to suggest that these gods were identified with the 400 brothers killed by the Aztec's national god Huitzilopochtli (see pages 100–101) when he burst from his mother's womb.

One of the gods of pulque, known by the date-name Two Rabbit, was especially revered in the vicinity of the birthplace of the last Aztec emperor, Motecuhzoma. The brutality and humiliation of the conquest had driven many Aztecs to the solace of pulque, which made the Spanish anxious to stamp out drunkenness. Assuming that Two Rabbit was the demon of intoxication, they smashed his image wherever they found it.

Although pulque, or *octli*, was sacred and used in many rituals, at the same time it was perceived by the Aztecs themselves as subversive. In the *Florentine Codex,* Father Bernardino de Sahagún recorded that even though "the god was wine, he was considered to be full of sin. For the god hurled people off crags, he strangled people, he drowned people, he killed them. He was an awesome being, one not to be affronted, one not to be abused." Drink had to be taken with due care. This suspicion of pulque was reflected in civil legislation. The sale of the drink was strictly regulated, and only certain people – the sick, the nobility and those over fifty-two years of age – were allowed regular access to it. Three cups per day was the prescribed ration. Adults found drunk three times in a row would on the first offence have their hair cut off, on the second offence have their houses demolished, and on the third be put to death.

Pulque was also freely used on ritual occasions, administered as a drug to prisoners who were going to be sacrificed. The prisoners, known as "children of the sun", were marched into Aztec territory in long, weary columns. They were forced to drink pulque until they were drunk; then made to dance and sing as they entered the great city of Tenochtitlan.

Mayahuel, entertained by a dancer, nestles in an agave cactus. Above them a jar of pulque floats in the night sky, below her an ascetic dances under a serpent. A detail from the Codex Borbonicus.

Lord of the Smoking Mirror

Among the first four gods created by Ometeotl in the thirteenth Heaven (see pages 58–59) was Black Tezcatlipoca. This restless, dark deity was described as "all-powerful and unequalled" and he could "see into the hearts of everyone".

"Tezcatlipoca", wrote Bernardino de Sahagún under the instruction of his Aztec informants, "was considered a true god, whose abode was every-where – in the land of the dead, on Earth and in Heaven." So impressed was de Sahagún with the stature of Tezcatlipoca, that he compared him to Jupiter, king of the gods in Roman mythology. Undoubtedly, Tezcatlipoca – as Black Tezcatlipoca was usually known – was quite unlike the Christian God worshipped by the con-quistadors. "When Tezcatlipoca walked on the Earth," continued de Sahagún, "he quickened vice and sin. He introduced anguish and affliction."

So different was the Aztec "Jupiter" from the Christian deity that de Sahagún described him as the opponent of God: "This wicked Tezcatlipoca we know as Lucifer, the great devil who there in the midst of Heaven, even at the beginning, began war, vice and filth." de Sahagún then succinctly summarized Tezcatlipoca's nature: "He created, he brought down all things." Tezcatlipoca, then, was the great god who could both create and destroy; he could bestow wealth, long life and happiness and then casually take them all away.

Among the most evocative and inscrutable aspects of Tezcatlipoca was his name, which meant "Smoking Mirror". The god carried one mirror at the back of his head and sometimes a second mirror replaced one of his feet, torn off when he was hurled out of Heaven for seducing a virgin goddess. The history of Tezcatlipoca's mir-ror is as obscure as the images in its smoking sur-face. But mirrors clearly had magical qualities. Toltec legend talks of a mirror, whose surface was like smoke, that could predict the end of droughts. Tezcatlipoca is said to have stolen this mirror and hidden it, thus prolonging the famine. The mirror "smoked" because it was made of obsidian, a black volcanic glass that reflects darkly and often with distortions. Tezcatlipoca could see into the future with his mirror and into people's hearts. This magical clairvoyance, that he alone of the gods possessed, made him patron of shamans, for whom mirrors were tools of the trade.

The Warrior God

Tezcatlipoca was vividly illustrated in the Aztec codices, where he was usually depicted as a warrior. Bearing the *atlatl* (spearthrower), darts and shield, he carried a war banner and wore in his hair the two heron feathers that were the usual headdress of the Aztec knights.

Tezcatlipoca had his opposite in both the gentler, life-giving Quetzalcoatl (see pages 74–75) and in the agricultural deity Red Tezcatlipoca or Xipe Totec (see pages 86–91). While Xipe was associated with the sun of the upper world, Black Tezcatlipoca represented the "dark sun" as it travelled at night through the Underworld. These opposing principles of day and night, light and darkness, were represented symbolically in the ballgame (see page 41) that was played throughout Mesoamerica. At the end of the Fifth Sun, this will be the game that Black Tezcatlipoca must win. For at the end of the present age Tezcatlipoca will steal the sun and thus destroy the world, the gods and human history.

Tezcatlipoca was also known as "The Left-handed One", implying that he was sinister and untrustworthy. Father de Sahagún described Tezcatlipoca in this guise as the god who "cast his shadow on one, visited one with the evils that befall men. He mocked, he ridiculed men."

Even more inauspiciously, the "left-handed" god was also known as Yaotl, the "Enemy" who stirred up discord and presided over battles. Social or political humiliation of any kind was attributed to Tezcatlipoca. He would do no one the favour of taking sides. Indeed, he was the promoter of wars and god of weaponry, and the insignia woven on his tunic was the skull and crossbones. Warriors who fell in battle would – unlike civilians – go to a temporary place of glory before they descended to the underworld (see page 126). But it was Tezcatlipoca who determined when and where they would fall. As god of battle, Tezcatlipoca performed a vital service to the entire Aztec pantheon, for it was only through war that a sufficient number of captives could be taken and transported to the temples of Tenochtitlan.

Tezcatlipoca's unpredictability was well illustrated by his association with certain animals. Many Aztec gods had a *nahualli*, or earthly double, often an animal whose character resembled their own. Tezcatlipoca excelled in assuming the form of his *nahualli*, and he was said to appear

This Aztec incense burner in the form of a turkey's claw, one of the symbols associated with Tezcatlipoca, is decorated with his sign.

71

The warrior god Tezcatlipoca wears a jaguar skin. Like the jaguar he was a creature to be feared, an implacable enemy and a fearsome fighter.

the most powerful and awe-inspiring wild creature in the region. The reason for this was clear to friar Bernardino de Sahagún, who described the jaguar as: "noble, princely, the ruler of animals. It is cautious, wide, proud. By night it watches. Very clear is its vision. Even when it is very dark, it sees." The spotted jaguar's skin, which Tezcatlipoca habitually wore, represented the night sky to the Aztecs. Just as the jaguar was the all-powerful creature of the night, merciless to its prey, so Tezcatlipoca was the darkest and most implacable deity in the whole pantheon.

Tezcatlipoca's darkness was emphasized in other ways. For example, he was often identified with the countless ghosts and spirits who haunted the night. Thus he appeared as a horrifying demon called Night Axe, a headless man with a wound in his chest that opened and shut with the slamming sound of an axe striking wood. The priests of Tezcatlipoca sometimes painted their bodies with a mixture of ground-up narcotic mushrooms, tobacco, poisonous snakes and scorpions, a weird black paste corresponding with the deity's own dark violence.

Virgin and Seducer

Tezcatlipoca was also conceived of as a beautiful young man, and was thus the presiding deity of youths training to become warriors. He was the

on Earth as a skunk, a monkey and a coyote: all of them sly, mischievous and deceitful creatures. But the animal most closely associated with Tezcatlipoca was the jaguar, and in his manifestation as One Jaguar, the god was compared with

youngest of the gods – sometimes described as a virgin, sometimes as an irresistible seducer of women – and in some versions of his story he was reborn every year. As Telpochtli, or "Young Male", Tezcatlipoca was worshipped by the *telpochtiliztli*, a sect of young men and women. In honour of the deity, these devotees would dress in sumptuous costumes at night and sing and dance through the streets of Tenochtitlan (see pages 122–123).

Although Tezcatlipoca was an unpredictable god who could bring misfortune and humble the successful, he also had his protective side. In one story, it was he who led the Aztecs in their search for a homeland. The dark god spurred them on by recounting the visions he could see in his super-natural mirror. Thus when the Aztecs arrived at Texcoco, across the water from their future capital of Tenochtitlan, the priests set up a mirror in Tezcatlipoca's temple, in which they saw the shadowy and beautiful visage of the deity himself.

Tezcatlipoca is dressed as an Aztec warrior in this 15th-century codex. He wears heron feathers in his hair, knee straps made of jaguar skin and carries a banner. His body is painted black and his face golden with black stripes.

The Origins of War

As a warrior god, one of Tezcatlipoca's most important functions for the Aztecs was to ensure that there was sufficient warfare to give them a steady supply of the captives they would need to sacrifice to the gods.

The Aztecs did not generally regard peace as a virtue. Their interest in political dominion over their neighbours and their devotion to gods of battle such as Tezcatlipoca led them rather to value the pursuit of war. But according to myth war had not always existed. Nor was it regarded as an indigenous Aztec practice. The Aztecs understood the pursuit of war to have come to them in early historical or mythological times from a remote north Mexican hunting people called the Chichimecs.

Far from feeling ashamed that they had not invented war for themselves, the Aztecs believed that to inherit a skill from such a venerable source gave it a sacred ancestry. As one text declared: "Could we betray the teaching of ancestors such as the Chichimecs or the Toltecs? No, our hearts have received life from them!"

The Aztecs explained the origins of war as a case of sibling rivalry between the children of the Sun and the Earth. The oldest brothers were loose-living and hard drinking, so the Sun and the Earth sent five younger brothers to sort them out. A war ensued in which the decadent older brothers were thrashed by the clean-living younger ones. The archetype of a puritan, ascetic warrior was born.

73

The Plumed Serpent

Quetzalcoatl, the "Plumed Serpent", was worshipped across Central Mexico and he was certainly one of the most revered gods in the Aztec pantheon. Like so many of his fellow deities he had several incarnations. The most important of these were as a creator god, one of the four sons of Ometeotl; as Ehecatl, the god of wind; as the Morning Star; and – uniquely among the gods – as a semi-human ruler, Topiltzin (see pages 76–79). The priestly Quetzalcoatl was often contrasted to his dark shamanic brother Tezcatlipoca. Throughout the myth cycle of the Aztecs the relations of the two brothers veer between enmity and alliance (see pages 60–63 and 76–79).

Quetzalcoatl's multifaceted character is suggested by the words that make up his compound name. While *quetzal*, meaning the quetzal bird's feather, refers to what is beautiful in Quetzalcoatl's nature, the word also means "precious". *Coatl*, the second part of the deity's name, also has a double meaning: "serpent" and "twin". The entire name could therefore mean both "Plumed Serpent" and "Precious Twin". This wordplay allowed the Mesoamericans to represent him sometimes as a snake with bright green feathers and sometimes in human form.

An Ancient God

Quetzalcoatl was one of the gods the Aztecs inherited from older civilizations in Mesoamerica. One of the earliest surviving representations of this great and exotic deity is at the third-century temple of Quetzalcoatl at Teotihuacan (see pages 110–111), which represented the point where Heaven and Earth met. This junction of the spheres, which Quetzalcoatl maintained, was necessary for the rain which brought agricultural prosperity to the Mexican plateau. Quetzalcoatl was associated with water, the sky – which the Aztecs believed was an extension of earthly waters (see page 58) – and, by extension, fertility and life itself. His power was regenerative and life-giving, because – to bring the rain – he linked the Earth with the sky. In one celebrated sculpture, Quetzalcoatl rises in great coils from a representation of the Earth Mother and joins the figure of Tlaloc, god of rain and lighting. Similarly, in his aspect as Ehecatl, the wind god, Quetzalcoatl was credited with the winds that brought rainclouds. In the *Vienna Codex*, he is shown as the wind god with his arms raised to support Heaven. Quetzalcoatl is thus holding up the clouds, and in his role as wind god is also blowing the rain across the thirsty lower world. In this guise, the god was known as "roadsweeper to the Tlaloques", the little rain gods, who lived in the mountains.

The Plumed Serpent devours a human being sacrificed in his honour, in a detail from the post-Conquest *Codex Borbonicus*.

Where Tezcatlipoca carried his obsidian mirror, in his guise as Ehecatl, the Plumed Serpent wore a conch shell, his symbolic "jewel of the wind". In imitation of their deity himself, priests of the Quetzalcoatl cult wore conch shells cut in cross section showing a concentric, whorled pattern that represented the movement of the wind. Many of the temples dedicated to Quetzalcoatl were also circular, signifying the eddying of the wind.

Quetzalcoatl was also often identified with one of the earliest of the Mexican deities: a dragon of the sky who could not only punish the human race with tornadoes and water spouts but also reward it by promoting agriculture. In this connection, Quetzalcoatl was also the beloved and ever-welcome deity of springtime and vegetation.

His primary connection with water was underlined in historical times when the conquistadors entered Quetzalcoatl's holy city of Cholula. During Aztec era, Cholula was a destination for pilgrims who came for advice or prognostication from the local priests. Poignantly, the people of Cholula were convinced that if Cortés and his men were to desecrate the temple of Quetzalcoatl, the lord of waters would create a huge flood and drown the invaders. They soon discovered their beliefs were unfounded.

God of Priestly Wisdom

The Aztecs also identified the Plumed Serpent with priesthood: the two most important priests in Tenochtitlan were given the title Quetzalcoatl, and the *calmecac* school where young priests were trained was also dedicated to him. In this incarnation, Quetzalcoatl was represented as a bearded man painted black. His attributes include a conical hat with a sharp projection, from which came a penitential blood offering to the god's *nahualli*, the quetzal bird.

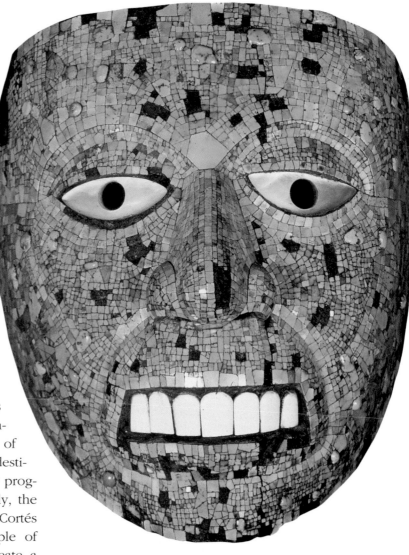

A mask – from around 1500 and decorated in turquoise and shell – represents Quetzalcoatl in human form. This type of mask was never intended to be worn over the face, but may have been worn elsewhere on the body. All Mesoamericans valued green materials – jade, turquoise or the green feathers of the quetzal bird – above any others. Cortés soon discovered this and bought Aztec gold in exchange for green glass beads.

In his semi-human incarnation, as the ruler Topiltzin, he was also high priest of Tula (see pages 76–79), initiating a peaceful, ascetic and spiritual era. His association with wise rulership meant that the green feathers of the quetzal bird or green stones were often worn as a sign of sovereignty by Mesoamerican rulers.

Tula's Golden Age

The figure of Quetzalcoatl the god merges in Mexican myth with a line of historical Toltec priest-kings known as "the Quetzalcoatls". One of their number was a pious reformer named Topiltzin, whose reign of peace and plenty in the sacred city of Tula, during the late ninth century AD, was fondly remembered by later generations.

An ancient Aztec poem laments the departure of a priestly king from his capital city in these words: "In Tula stood the house of beams, where still the serpent columns stand deserted. Gone away is Topiltzin. He is wept for by our princes!" The city of the "serpent columns" was a sacred ceremonial site idealized in Aztec history as the Toltec capital of Tula. As well as being associated in mythology with the god Quetzalcoatl, Tula was also an actual city. Its ruins (c.AD900–1200), dominated by the pyramid sacred to Quetzalcoatl, may be visited to this day in the Mexican state of Hidalgo.

The Toltec empire that had its political and ceremonial centre at Tula was a warrior state. For three centuries, it dominated the territory northeast of the later Mexican capital Tenochtitlan. One of its patron deities was the war god Tezcatlipoca (see pages 70–73), whom the Aztecs later incorporated into their own mythology. But at some stage in Toltec history, the cult of this ruthless warrior god was challenged, and perhaps even temporarily replaced, by the devotees of a gentler religion. The presiding deity of this new cult was Quetzalcoatl; the priest-kings who established his

worship were likewise called "the Quetzalcoatls". According to Aztec myth, the greatest of the Toltec priest-kings was Topiltzin. In the course of time, as Aztec knowledge of the Toltec era faded, Topiltzin was nevertheless remembered not simply as a great reforming king but became identified with the god Quetzalcoatl himself.

Here history and myth become inextricably intertwined. Topiltzin, says one source, appeared in the year One Reed, miraculously born after his mother had swallowed an emerald. In another story the priest-king is described as the child of Coatlicue, the Earth Mother (see pages 64–65). In yet another account Topiltzin was originally a warrior who undertook seven years of penance before becoming king of Tula, where he introduced an unprecedentedly pious and peace-loving regime.

Nothing is known for certain about the real history of Topiltzin. His name, meaning "Our Revered Prince", suggests that he was from the highest ranks of Toltec society. But whoever he was, the hero remembered as Quetzalcoatl-Topiltzin probably did inaugurate a new approach to the religious life. His preaching challenged the established tradition, as upheld by the warrior elite, of human sacrifice and the cult of Tezcatlipoca. Instead of human blood and hearts, claimed the new priesthood, the great god wanted offerings such as flowers, birds and butterflies.

A faction supporting the cult of Tezcatlipoca fiercely resisted this benign religion and the civil war that followed left them in control of Tula. The defeated Topiltzin led his followers and much of the city's population away to the Mexican Gulf coast. There the great priest died, while the city of Tula reverted to its old ways and the bloody and frightening rituals began again.

At Tula, these enormous columns representing warriors impressed the Aztecs but have convinced archaeologists that the Toltecs were in fact not a peaceful people.

Quetzalcoatl emerges from the jaws of a coyote in a sculpture from the Toltec site of Tula. After inheriting him from the Toltecs, the Aztecs invented their own myths about him.

The Legend Grows

As the story of the Toltec reformer receded in the collective memory, it was reconstructed in Aztec legend. Since the Plumed Serpent was of Toltec origin and had conferred on Toltec kings the divine right to rule, the Aztecs assumed that by adopting the same cult and assimilating with the Toltec elite they too could achieve an empire like their predecessors. Furthermore, they married off as many of their noblemen as they could to princesses of Toltec descent in order to improve their bloodline (see pages 96–99).

The hero of the Aztec legend, like the historical (or semi-historical) Topiltzin, was a civilized ascetic who led a religious revival involving prayer and penitence. The myth describes how the mysterious Topiltzin-Quetzalcoatl prepared himself by practising austerities for four years in the city of

Tulantzinco. There he instituted a priesthood and proclaimed the holy life, until the Toltecs of Tula petitioned him to bring his reforms to their city. In Tula, Topiltzin-Quetzalcoatl broadened the cult of Quetzalcoatl, abolishing human sacrifice, and eventually managed to win over the whole pantheon of Toltec deities as well as Tula's political and religious establishment.

A Blessed Era

A wondrous Golden Age followed. It was a period of religious fervour, when Topiltzin-Quetzalcoatl's laws were proclaimed from the city's hills. It was also a magical era of plenty. Gourds, chillis and cotton grew in abundance. Ears of maize were so large that they could only be picked up in one's arms. Cotton grew ready-dyed in a rainbow of different colours – "red, yellow, pale rose, violet, green, deep blue, verdigris, ivory, brown, shadowy, rose red and coyote-coloured". Brightly coloured birds – "the blue continga, the quetzal, the troupial, the red spoonbill and many others" – spoke clearly and sang sweetly.

Topiltzin-Quetzalcoatl's rule also saw high artistic achievement in stone, gold and other precious materials. In fact, the people of Tula invented all the major technologies of Mesoamerica during this period: "There were scribes, jewellers, stone cutters, carpenters, masons, potters, spinners, weavers and miners."

Tula was also a great ceremonial centre. Here was devised the Mesoamerican calendar which showed the Toltecs "which day-sign was good and which was evil". Tula's priests were the first diviners of the future and interpreters of dreams. The people of Tula also "understood the stars" and gave them names. Their priests were so powerful that they penetrated the heavens to receive knowledge directly from the supreme being Ometeotl.

The great temples built during this Golden Age had high jewelled walls. Topiltzin-Quetzalcoatl himself had many palaces made of precious things, including one made of brilliantly coloured feathers.

During Tula's golden age Topiltzin-Quetzalcoatl led his people in penances that included fasting, setting thorns in the flesh, ritual

bleeding and midnight ablutions in freezing water. "But", as the *Florentine Codex* remarks, "at last Quetzalcoatl and the Toltecs became neglectful."

The Fall of the King

Stories conflict about how Topiltzin-Quetzalcoatl's reign ended, but the opposition to Tula's priestly dispensation now crystallized around Tezcatlipoca. One account tells how Tezcatlipoca came down from Heaven on a rope of woven spider's silk and, during a ballgame with Quetzalcoatl, transformed himself into an ocelot and drove the god-priest back to his original city of Cholula. Another story recounts how the dark warrior deity appeared to Topiltzin-Quetzalcoatl with his convex mirror and the god-priest saw himself distorted in its depths.

Another tale tells how, as Topiltzin-Quetzalcoatl lay sick, an avatar of Tezcatlipoca tried to gain access to him in the form of a white-haired old man. Topiltzin-Quetzalcoatl's attendants tried to turn the unholy visitor away, but the divine priest insisted on seeing him. Asking after Topiltzin-Quetzalcoatl's health, the visitor found that the god-priest was weary: "All tired is my body, as if undone." The old man offered Topiltzin-Quetzalcoatl a potion, promising that it would both intoxicate and refresh him: "You will weep; you will be compassionate. You will think of your death. You will be as a child again."

The drink was pulque, and at first Topiltzin-Quetzalcoatl resisted the temptation. But eventually his resolve broke down and he drank the pulque and became drunk. It is difficult to tell from the story as recorded exactly what happened next. But some scholars believe that in a drunken state Topiltzin-Quetzalcoatl seduced his own sister. This terrible crime marked his final defeat. The Golden Age drew to a close: the god-priest set about burning his beautiful city and hiding its precious works of art. He sent the birds away and changed the cacao trees to mesquites. When he was finished he set out on a journey.

One myth says that Topiltzin-Quetzalcoatl sacrificed himself, his heart rising to become the Morning Star (see page 82–83). Another says that he stepped on to a raft made of serpents and was carried to the mythical city of Tlapallan.

CHICHEN ITZA

The greatest city of Mesoamerica's Postclassic era, Chichen Itza in Mexico's Yucatán peninsula puzzles and intrigues scholars to this day. As its name indicates, it was the headquarters of the Itza, a people who apparently found their way to it from the Maya heartland to the south. But its architectural details, including a penchant for death's head decorations (*right*), show a marked similarity to those of the Toltec capital of Tula in the Valley of Mexico hundreds of kilometres to the north-west. Some scholars have suggested that it was occupied by a Toltec faction driven from Tula (*see page 98*); but others maintain that the Itza must already have been in close contact with the northern civilization, citing the superior workmanship of Chichen Itza's architecture to argue that Tula's builders copied from it. What all can agree on is that the city is one of Mesoamerica's finest sites, displaying in its architecture a fusion of northern and southern styles that enriches both traditions.

Below: The round building known today as the Caracol, or "snail', dominates this view of Chichen Itza's ceremonial centre. The windows in the upper section are thought to have been used for astronomical observations of the planet Venus.

Above: Columns, including this cluster in the Temple of the Warriors, are distinctive to Chichen Itza. Unknown at earlier Maya sites, they show influences from the Valley of Mexico.

Below: A stone *chacmool* reclines outside the Temple of the Warriors. A bowl on the figure's stomach would once have received sacrificial offerings.

Left: One of the four monumental stairways which mount the pyramid known as El Castillo to a square temple positioned on its summit. Each staircase has 91 steps; an extra tread at the entrance to the stone sanctuary brings the total to 365, the number of days in the solar year.

Quetzalcoatl as the Morning Star

One story tells how Quetzalcoatl, in his manifestation as the priest-king Topiltzin, sacrificed himself at the end of his reign. Weeping, he arrayed himself in all his finery including his turquoise mask; then he stepped on to a pyre and lit it. As his body was consumed by flames, his heart rose into the sky to become the Morning Star. From his new place in the heavens, Quetzalcoatl promised that one day he would to return to Earth and establish a lasting era of peace and harmony.

This winged image of Quetzalcoatl as the Morning Star was recorded soon after the Conquest. The resemblance to a Christian angel may have been deliberate.

Quetzalcoatl was a truly protean deity. Worshipped as both the Plumed Serpent and the god of the wind, he was also identified with the Morning Star under the name of Ce Acatl. The Morning Star, or Venus when it rises befor the sun, was known to the Aztecs as "Lord of the Time of Dawn"; as a competitor to the sun – which rose when Venus faded – he was regarded with awe.

This mistrust of Venus derived from the deep antagonism in Aztec myth between light and darkness. Because the stars – even those which appear at dawn – represented the night sky, Ce Acatl and the sun were believed to be hostile to one another. Since the sun was obviously vital to life on Earth, the Morning Star was therefore regarded as inauspicious. Old people, children and rulers were particularly vulnerable to his anger. Paradoxically, while Quetzalcoatl in his aspect as the wind god was adored as the harbinger of rain, Ce Acatl in his dawn dominion was the enemy of rain and the bringer of drought.

But like so many other Mesoamerican deities Ce Acatl embodied a paradox: the mistrust was often mingled with gratitude. Although on the one hand the Morning Star was notorious for having assaulted, in his guise as the god of cold, the first sun to rise after the auto-sacrifice of the gods (see pages 84–85); on the other hand it was believed that the star also helped lift the sun on its journey into the sky each morning.

Despite these ambiguities, the myth of Quetzalcoatl's exile from Tula and his ascent into the sky to become the Morning Star was widely thought to prophesy a happy future, a prospect to which the Aztecs clung. This promise was contained in Quetzalcoatl's own prediction before his death that he would one day return, conquer his enemies and establish a new dominion of piety.

Quetzalcoatl's Ominous Return

As Cortés was making his way through Mexico towards Tenochtitlan, the Aztecs believed that this strange new figure was none other than Quetzalcoatl himself, returning to bring in a new era of peace and prosperity. In one of history's most bizarre coincidences, Cortés arrived in the city on the very day, One Reed, prophesied for the return of Quetzalcoatl. The Aztecs and other Mesoamerican peoples adopted Christianity quickly. Many seem to have believed that it was simply another version of the rites of Quetzalcoatl.

There seem to have been two main reasons for this eagerness to convert. Firstly, according to Cortés' companion Bernal Diaz, the Spanish missionaries resembled in appearance the Aztec priests of Tenochtitlan, who "wore black cloaks like cassocks and long gowns reaching to their feet. Some had hoods like those worn by canons, and others had smaller hoods like those of the Dominicans." More importantly, the Christian message of brotherly love seemed to be paralleled by the ideals of piety and good government represented by Quetzalcoatl in his aspect as the priestly ruler Topiltzin.

The story of Christ's death and resurrection was a further echo of the Aztec belief in Quetzalcoatl's second coming. In this way Jesus and the Mesoamerican deity became identified as one holy being. So while much of Aztec culture and religion was swept away by the onslaught of the Spanish conquistadors, the worship of the Plumed Serpent managed to survive, though in a barely recognizable form.

Quetzalcoatl in his guise as the Morning Star bursts out of the Earth, represented by a serpent, in this pre-Toltec stone carving.

The Creation of the Sun and Moon

Two gods of vastly different characters, Tecuciztecatl and Nanahuatzin – one all vanity and one all humility – are central to Aztec myth because they were to transform themselves into the lesser deity of the moon and the all-powerful god of the sun.

The creation of the sun and moon took place at the great ceremonial centre of Teotihuacan, about 40 kilometres northeast of Mexico City. After the fourth holocaust, in which the sun as well as the Earth had been annihilated, four gods met in the darkness at Teotihuacan to create a new sun. They agreed that the self-sacrifice of a god was required to bring it into being.

As the gods discussed who should die by fire to create the new sun, the vain and handsome Tecuciztecatl put himself forward "to carry the burden, to bring the dawn". But the gods decided to make him compete with the god Nanahuatzin for the position of sun or moon. Although an equally powerful god, Nanahuatzin was very humble, maybe because he was disfigured by running sores.

While the gods built a vast sacrificial bonfire, Tecuciztecatl and Nanahuatzin did penance on two mounds. The two gods now presented offerings that reflected their personalities. Where vain, boastful Tecuciztecatl brought quetzal feathers and gold, Nanahuatzin brought bunches of reeds. Where Tecuciztecatl offered awls of coral and jade, Nanahuatzin merely offered cactus spines anointed with his own blood.

Tecuciztecatl Fails

When, after four days, the sacrificial fire had become searingly hot, the two gods were robed for their ordeal: Tecuciztecatl in the richest garments, Nanahuatzin in a tunic of paper. The attendant gods, still taken in by Tecuciztecatl's pretensions, now called upon him to jump into the fire.

Tecuciztecatl ran towards the flames, but four times recoiled in terror from the intolerable heat. So the gods called on Nanahuatzin: "Daring, determined, resolved and with hardened heart, he shut his eyes. He did not falter or turn back. All at once he threw himself into the fire. His body crackled and sizzled; he burned." Spurred on by Nanahuatzin's heroic act, Tecuciztecatl too ran into the pyre. The gods now waited in the darkness for the birth of the new sun. But instead Tecuciztecatl rose as the moon, casting a blinding light. To subdue his brilliance, one of the gods threw a rabbit up into his face. This rabbit can still be seen on the face of the full moon.

Nanahuatzin now rose in the heavens as the new sun, but refused to move across the sky until he had been fed with the hearts and blood of all the other deities. Incensed at this demand, the Morning Star attacked the sun with his darts and spear, only to be defeated and hurled down into the Underworld. The sun god was acknowledged as supreme, and all 1,600 gods now allowed themselves to be sacrificed.

The humble, ulcerated Nanahuatzin was thus transformed into the mighty sun god Tonatiuh, he "who blinded one with his light". The first day of the Fifth Sun had begun.

Birthplace of the Gods

The name Teotihuacan means the "Place where God was Created". The Aztecs, who only knew it as ruins, believed this city of plazas, palaces and pyramids in Central Mexico was the very place where the Fifth Sun itself was created. They were awed by the evidence of a once great civilization that had been utterly lost.

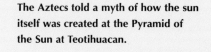

The Aztecs told a myth of how the sun itself was created at the Pyramid of the Sun at Teotihuacan.

Indeed, Teotihuacan was also said to have been where the whole pantheon of Aztec gods was brought into being. The *Florentine Codex* of Bernardino de Sahagún confirms that the Aztecs made it their first sacred centre when they arrived after their long journey from the north in search of a final home. At Teotihuacan the newcomers made offerings to the gods who had led them to safety, buried their leaders and built pyramids above their tombs.

Another Aztec legend claims that Teotihuacan's famous pyramids of the Sun and Moon (see pages 110–111) are the very mounds on which the gods Tecuciztecatl and Nanahuatzin did penance before sacrificing themselves to the flames and becoming the moon and sun.

Gods of the Natural World

Of the many gods of the Mexican pantheon, none could match the popular appeal of those associated with the fertility of the land. To a primarily agricultural people, the harvest rather than conquest was the sign of the gods' munificence.

While intellectuals sought to explain the mysteries of the universe through cosmological speculation and in terms of sun and star deities, the mass of the population were more concerned with the gods whose activities touched their daily lives. In particular, concerns about drought and the fertility of the land lay at the heart of day-to-day Mesoamerican religion, while the 360-day calendar (see pages 114–115) was planned around the agricultural year, which began in February.

Mexico's climate is marked by long seasons of torrential rain followed by very dry seasons, so the propitiation of the rain gods was considered essential. The chief rain god was Tlaloc. But reflecting its importance, many other lesser deities were associated with rain or water. A whole host of gods were also linked to agriculture and in particular

with maize. Different gods represented different stages of its development; for example Xipe Totec, the "Flayed One", was associated with the first shoots of maize in spring, while growing maize was celebrated with a big midsummer festival to the maize goddess Xilonen, during which everyone feasted on maize porridge, tamales and tortillas wrapped around chillied vegetables.

These preoccupations with the natural world show through in one of history's sadder public statements, made when leading Aztec priests were informed after the Conquest that they would have to abandon their old beliefs. Disputing the

The Earth Mother, pictured centre, nourishes a tree with her being, represented by flowing blue lines in this mural from around the eighth century at Teotihuacan.

decision, they tried to explain just what their vast and complex pantheon meant to them and to their people. "It is through the gods that all live," they informed the Franciscan missionaries who brought them the news; "they give us our daily fare and all that we drink, all that we eat, our sustenance, maize, beans, amaranth. It is they who we supplicate for water, for rain with which everything flourishes on the Earth."

This last reference was an eloquent one, for the most actively venerated figure in the Aztec world was the rain god Tlaloc. He is easily recognized in the codices, as much for his round goggle eyes as for the insignia associated with him: in one hand he holds a jade tomahawk symbolizing a thunderbolt or the writhing serpent of lightning, while in the other he carries a jug from which he pours out the rain. His other distinctive feature is his jaguar teeth, a connection that may have been suggested by a perceived resemblance between the sound of thunder rumbling and the big cat snarling.

Tlaloc was revered as an old god, with a long history behind him (see page 17); the earliest known image of him comes from a vase made in the Valley of Mexico as far back as the first century BC. He was an important figure at Teotihuacan, featuring prominently among the culture's leading deities. In Aztec mythology he was remembered as the being who presided over the Third Sun of creation, when he ruled a world of rain that was eventually destroyed by a hail of fiery cinders.

"She of the Jade Skirt", Tlaloc's consort, made the plants grow. This Aztec stone sculpture depicts her in her youthful incarnation as mistress of childbirth and the spring.

Mistress of Torrents and Whirlpools

While Tlaloc had responsibility for water as it fell from the sky, his consort Chalchiuhtlicue – the "She of the Jade Skirt" – was the presiding spirit of rivers, lakes and other places where rain is collected. She too had ruled over one of the ages of creation – in her case the Fourth Sun, the Sun of Water. As a goddess associated with growth and the beginnings of life, Chalchiuhtlicue played a significant role in the rituals surrounding the birth

of babies. In particular, she presided over a rite that fascinated Spanish churchmen because of its resemblance to baptism. A priest sprinkled water over a newly born infant to cleanse it of the spiritual uncleanliness passed down from its parents. The child was given its name and presented with miniature tools that symbolized the occupations it might take up in later life.

An imposing figure dressed in blue and white with a crown of blue reeds, Chalchiuhtlicue was by no means always the placid figure a connection with lakes and ponds might suggest. Known sometimes as the "Agitated" or "Foaming One", she was also associated with whirlpools and

Cults of the Jaguar

The jaguar was the top predator of the Mesoamerican rainforest. Feared for its nocturnal hunting skills, it became a symbol of silent power that kings and even gods sought to emulate.

A god emerges from the jaws of a jaguar in this Zapotec image from the sixth century.

From the start of Mesoamerican civilization, in the religion of the Olmecs, the jaguar played an important role. Images of were-Jaguars – humans with the power to transform themselves into the beast – suggest that the connection may have gone back into the shamanistic practices of even earlier times.

In later years, the cult of the jaguar was strongest among the Maya, who inhabited the southern jungle lands where the animal lived. Among their gods was a Jaguar Baby, resembling the snarling infant figure common in Olmec art.

In the northern kingdoms of the Valley of Mexico region, the jaguar was equally respected, even though few of their citizens could ever have seen one. Teotihuacan had a Temple of the Jaguars, so called from depictions of the animal on its walls. The mysterious image of a netted jaguar also figured prominently in the city's religious symbolism.

One of the two great Aztec military orders was that of the Jaguar Knights. But the animal's main association in later times was with Tezcatlipoca, who often took the form of a jaguar. Silent, nocturnal and deadly, the great cat was in every way a fitting symbol for the most formidable of all the gods.

A harvest feast whose main dish is a meal
of cooked maize is celebrated in honour of
the god Quetzalcoatl, in a detail from a
pre-Conquest Aztec codex.

The tlaloques also play a significant part in an Aztec myth that tells how maize was first given to the world. In the beginning the grain was known only to red ants, who kept it hidden deep inside Mount Tonacatepetl, a prominent local peak. To find out what they were concealing, Quetzalcoatl transformed himself into a black ant and made his way unseen to their secret storeroom. He took samples of the cereal back to the other gods, who tasted it and found that it was delicious. Chewing it into a mash, they placed it in the mouths of human babies, and discovered that it was just the food that the human race needed to grow up healthy and strong. But the rest of the store still had to be recovered from its hiding place if people were to benefit from its nourishment. To release it, Quetzalcoatl slung a rope round the mountain and tried to shift it, but it was too heavy for him. Perplexed, the gods took the problem to Oxomoco and Cipactonal, the divine couple who were the oldest of all the gods. They decreed that Nanahuatzin, the creator of the Fifth Sun, should be given the task of splitting the mountain open. He did so with the help of the tlaloques, who snatched up the grain inside and scattered it – and so were responsible for bringing the crop to humankind.

Altogether eight of the twenty monthly festivals in honour of the gods were dedicated to those associated with water, either directly – as in the case of the festival of Tozoztontli when flowers were offered to Tlaloc – or indirectly. These water festivals started in February and carried on until November. They included the festival of the salt goddess Uixtocihuatl, sister of the rain gods,

torrents. Representations show her seated on a throne from which a raging flood surges forth, sometimes carrying struggling humans away.

Living at high altitude, the Aztecs associated rivers with mountains, which they considered to be the home of rain. Tlaloc himself lived on a peak to the east of the Valley of Mexico that bears his name to this day. On its summit, more than 4,000 metres up, stood a shrine to the god. Those heights were also the homes of the god's attendants, the tlaloques. Sometimes there were said to be many of these, but on other occasions just five were shown, each bringing a different kind of rain: fiery rain (possibly symbolizing drought), fungus rain, wind rain, beneficial rain symbolized by jade signs, and flint-blade rain, which was probably a reference to violent hail. Like Tlaloc himself, they were widely venerated and it seems likely that they were very popular. People made gruelling pilgrimages to visit the caves where they were supposed to dwell. Sometimes children were sacrificed to them, immured in caverns behind huge boulders. The priests who abandoned them there believed they were committing them to an earthly paradise in the heart of the mountain.

Macuilxochitl, god of gambling, challenges a few mortals to the game of patolli, "the game of the mat", in a detail from a 15th-century codex. According to the Spanish, the Aztecs were inveterate gamblers.

in June – when old women and young girls wearing flowers in their hair danced together. In September, Tepeilhuitl – the festival in honour of the mountains where clouds gather – was celebrated by making dough sculptures of mountains. Those who had passed away and gone to the drizzly jungle paradise presided over by Tlaloc (see page 127) were remembered at this time.

Gods of Maize

A whole body of legend surrounded maize, Mesoamerica's staple crop, and a cluster of divinities shared responsibility for its growth and fruition. Maya maize gods had elongated heads that recalled the shape of ears of the cereal; it is possible that people may even have deformed the skulls of infants in imitation of them.

By Aztec days at least four separate deities were associated with the maize plant in different aspects of its growth. In its earliest stage, the tender green ear was symbolized by Xilonen, conceived of as a dancing maiden with a double ear of the cereal in each hand. There was also a male personification of the young plant in the shape of

Cinteotl, a young man coloured yellow in the codices and sporting sheaves of maize in his headdress. The goddess of the harvested crop was Chicomecoatl, who received the gratitude of the populace for her bounty every August.

Cinteotl, maize's masculine personification, was closely associated in the people's minds with various other young male deities associated with sensual pleasure, the connection apparently lying in a link perceived between the fertility of the land and human sexuality.

One was Xochipilli, literally, "Flower Prince". Portrayed as a handsome youth beating on a drum, he was the patron of flowers, dancing, feasting and all occasions on which people wore garlands on their heads. Less happily, he was also responsible for inflicting boils, haemorrhoids and venereal diseases on individuals guilty of sexual excess. Another young god associated both with pleasure and the penalties of excess was Macuilxochitl, patron of games and gambling.

Perhaps, the oddest of all the deities associated with the growing crop, however, was Xipe Totec, a god of springtime honoured when the maize seed first sprouted. For reasons still not fully understood, but most likely connected with a myth that is now lost, he was known as the "Flayed One", and victims were sacrificed to him in particularly bizarre and gory ways.

Some were tied to frames and shot with arrows, their blood being allowed to drip onto a round stone that symbolized the Earth. Others were condemned to the so-called "gladiatorial sacrifice", in which captive warriors wielding mock weapons edged with feathers fought fully armed Aztec knights. After

they had duly bled to death from the wounds they received, the prisoners' bodies were flayed. Their captors then wore the skins, tied over their own naked flesh, for twenty days, during which time they ran around the city begging for alms. The religious symbolism behind this startlingly gruesome exercise apparently invoked the way in which maize seeds lose their old skin when the new growth bursts forth, and therefore it was associated with the beginning of a new cycle.

Xipe Totec, a god of regeneration, often wore a human skin, in imitation of the way maize seeds wear a husk. This Aztec granite mask shows him as a fresh-faced young man.

The Mixtec Codices

Through the survival of four pre-Conquest codices, scholars have traced the history of the Mixtecs farther back than any other Mesoamerican people aside from the Maya. As well as telling the story of their own rise to power in the Valley of Oaxaca, the codices recorded myths, though mostly in pictorial form. In 1607, a Spanish friar, Gregorio Garcia, wrote some of these as narrative, giving us two versions of some Mixtec myths.

From about AD900, a cluster of small but powerful kingdoms occupied the dry, barren hills and lush, fertile valleys of the Mexican region of Mixteca. Right up until the Spanish Conquest, these kingdoms, united by language, beliefs and political alliances, maintained a lofty independence, evading absorption into the mighty Aztec empire to the north and, using a combination of aggression and diplomacy, themselves overrunning the Zapotecan homelands.

The Mixtec creator gods Lord and Lady One Deer in a detail from the *Vienna Codex*, which was painted at the height of Mixtec power and is the chief source of information about their mythology.

Their pre-Conquest codices were of folding deerskin, written partly in phonetic script and partly in hieroglyphic "puzzle writing". Covering a 600-year time span, from about AD940, the books were written for the Mixtec nobility, describing in detail the genealogies of the ruling class. Together with the archaeological evidence, these precious codices suggest that Mixtec political history and indigenous myth were intertwined.

Like other peoples in Mesoamerica, the Mixtecs believed in a multitude of gods. These gods' powers were never entirely distinct from the worldly powers of the Mixtec nobility. Indeed, the same terms were often used to refer both to rulers on Earth and the deities who moved between Earth and heaven. As a result, the codices often describe the birth of the ancestors of noble Mixtec dynasties as if they were supernatural beings who had sprung from the Earth, from trees and stones, or even from heaven. Mixtec kings were so closely identified with their terrestrial kingdoms that some were also said to have originated from the very signs in the codices that represented plants or places within Mixtec territory. Nobles also had a sacred legislative function. They were originators of doctrine and also Bearers of the Holy Bundle, a sacred object presented by a god to represent him on Earth.

The Creation Myth

The first beings were an ancient couple who lived in a timeless darkness. They gave birth to a younger pair called Lord and Lady One Deer, who had many children. Two of these children made a beautiful and fragrant garden which they filled with roses and flowering trees. In one version of the creation myth, the first Mixtecs were born from a tree in this garden. In another, the first Mixtec people were believed to have emerged from a tree at a place called Apoala in the province of Mixteca Alta. From this centre the first nobles scattered in the four cardinal directions. At each of these four points they established their kingdoms, naming the

Earth, Sky and Rain

The Mixtecs thought of the cosmos as having two halves: the Earth, which was female, and the sky, which was male and consisted of water. Rain, essential to agriculture in the arid conditions of southern Mexico, was an expression of life-generating sexual relations between the Earth and Sky.

Earth and sky were not always separate. In the dark beginnings of time, they were one, and the Earth itself was simply mud and slime. The division of the cosmos occurred when a culture hero, Lord Nine Wind, raised the waters of the sky from the Earth's surface. Into the mist and slime of primordial Earth before time began and the Mixtec people had constructed their 260-day calendar, two other deities appeared. The male god was One Deer "Lion-Serpent" and the beautiful female god was One Deer "Jaguar-Serpent". As the similarity of their names implies, these deities were essentially male and female aspects of one another. They were the parents of all the later gods, and built an immense and luxurious palace near Apoala to house the gods on Earth. On the roof of their own palace was a copper axe, the edge turned upwards, on which the sky rested.

places within them, building temples and initiating all the ceremonies that would dominate civil and religious life.

Historical Mixtec rulers used these myths of origin in order to legitimate their claims to authority. The early codices explained that these ancient kings, while enjoying divine powers of their own, were in frequent communication with the gods. For example, before his accession to the Mixtec throne, Lord Eight Wind was bathed by the rain god as an initiation to power.

The rain god dives from heaven in a flash of lightning and pours sacred water to bless the new king, Lord Eight Wind.

THE PEOPLE OF FIRE AND RAIN

The Aztecs were latecomers on the Mesoamerican stage. At the start of the 14th century AD, when the Renaissance was starting a world away in Italy, they were a small nomadic tribe known as the Mexica – the name from which the word Mexico would eventually be derived. It was 1325 before they founded their capital, Tenochtitlan, and another hundred years before they established an empire. Less than a century later they were swept away by Spanish guns. As for the word "Aztec" itself, that was to come even later – coined by nineteenth-century historians to describe the civilization the Mexica had created in alliance with neighbouring peoples.

In the long saga of Mesoamerican history, the Aztecs' glory was short lived, a comet-like progress casting a brief but brilliant light. In view of their ephemerality, it is maybe not surprising that their particular contribution to the mythology of the region was small. For the most part they were content, like other peoples around them, to honour the gods of those who had gone before. They shared the deities and the beliefs of the region as a whole.

Yet there were a few purely Aztec myths, and for the most part they related directly to the Mexicas' rise to imperial might. The story of the tribe's early wanderings became a heroic odyssey in which verifiable historical fact meshed inextricably with supernatural fiction. In the divine sphere, the tribal god Huitzilopochtli grew in importance to occupy a central role in the Mesoamerican pantheon. His worship was even imposed on conquered peoples brought by force into the Aztec fold.

To accommodate the newcomer, some readjustment of the roles and functions of the longer-established Mesoamerican deities was required. Huitzilopochtli's cult had solar aspects that in many ways encroached on the sphere of the region's established sun god, Tonatiuh. But such overlapping seems to have caused the Aztecs themselves little concern. Their general approach was syncretistic – an attitude symbolized by the joint dedication of the Great Temple of Tenochtitlan to Huitzilopochtli and the most venerable of all Mesoamerican divinities, the rain god Tlaloc.

Above: Quetzalcoatl in his guise of wind god carries a giant shell and a wind trumpet mask; near him flutters a quetzal bird in this detail from the *Codex Magliabechiano*.

Left: This vessel in the shape of the mask of the rain god Tlaloc, painted a brilliant blue, was found at the site of the Tenochtitlan's Central Temple. It may have been used to catch rainwater as part of an agricultural ritual.

In Search of a Homeland

Even though the Aztec empire was barely a century old when it was struck down, its origins were already fading into myth. Blending historical fact with legend, the epic tale of the arrival of the empire's founders in the Valley of Mexico was recorded for posterity by chroniclers after the Conquest.

The Aztecs called the country from which the Mexica set out on their journey Aztlan or "Place of Cranes", a word from which their own name would eventually be derived. They thought of this homeland as lying on a lake island somewhere to the northwest of their eventual resting place at Tenochtitlan on Lake Texcoco. In recent years, historians have made inconclusive attempts to locate the Place of Cranes, linking it with various sites in northern Mexico from Lake Patzcuaro, less than 250 kilometres to the west of Mexico City, to lagoons in the state of Nayarit 800 kilometres away.

As it happens, their curiosity was shared by the Aztecs themselves. In the 1440s, when the empire was in its first great phase of expansion, Motecuhzoma I despatched an expedition of 60 holy men in search of the site. The travellers made their way to the reputed birthplace of the tribal god, Huitzilopochtli. From there they set off in search of the lost island by shamanistic soul-flight – transformed into the shape of birds, as the texts would have it. On their return to Tenochtitlan, they reported that they had duly reached their destination, where they found Nahuatl-speaking people paddling canoes. Better still, they had met Huitzilopochtli's mother, Coatlicue. She warned them that, just as they had vanquished other peoples, so one day they would be conquered themselves.

When they first left Aztlan, the tribe meandered through the dry lands of northern Mexico before taking up temporary residence inside a mountain which they called Chicomoztoc – literally Seven Caves. Here the story plunges into pure myth, for it was the common claim of almost all formerly nomadic Mesoamerican peoples to have emerged into the world from Chicomoztoc's womb-like caves. According to modern mythographers, the story symbolizes a conversion to agriculture, after which the

An expedition of holy men searching for the Aztec homeland ran into Coatlicue – depicted here in her guise as "She of the Serpent Skirt". She warned them that the Aztecs would one day be vanquished.

The Heavenly Huntsman

Portrayed with a bow and arrow and a net for collecting game, the hunter Mixcoatl was the patron god of the nomad invaders of the Valley of Mexico and of all who claimed descent from them.

Mixcoatl wears bodypaint associated with warriors who are to be sacrificed, in this detail from an Aztec codex.

Mixcoatl first rose to prominence among the Toltecs. Legend had it that it was he who brought the Toltecs to the city of Tula and fathered Topiltzin, their semi-mythical ruler (see pages 76–79).

In myth, Mixcoatl was the father of Quetzalcoatl but was also linked with the Plumed Serpent's enemy, Tezcatlipoca. Mixcoatl also had a place in the heavens, where he was associated with the Milky Way. His name, which meant Cloud Serpent, may have been a poetic reference to that starry band. As such, he personified the souls of sacrificed warriors, who were believed to be transformed into stars after death.

Mixcoatl received sacrifices of a particularly unpleasant kind. The month of the Aztec calendar sacred to him was marked by ritual hunts, and at the festival that marked its climax a woman victim was despatched like a hunted animal. Her head was struck against a rock four times to stun her, then her throat was cut and she was decapitated. A male victim displayed the head to the watching crowd before his own heart was cut out and offered to the god.

tribes were "reborn" into a new relationship with the Earth. Illustrations of Chicomoztoc show the Seven Caves radiating in clover-leaf fashion off a central chamber.

Excavations in 1971 at the site of the city of Teotihuacan, destroyed 500 years before the Mexica set out on their travels, revealed just such a cavity inside the Pyramid of the Sun. The find suggested that the concept of birth from the Earth's womb had significance for the entire region. Its influence may even have stretched further afield, for Maya legend too spoke of a place of the same name; the Quiché people supposedly went to "Seven Caves" to receive their tribal god.

For the Mexica, the next destination was Coatepec, the Hill of the Snake, located near the Toltec capital of Tula. This place retained great significance for the Aztecs, as the story of Motecuhzoma's mission shows, for it was there that Huitzilopochtli was said to have been born (see page 100). In later times the Great Temple at Tenochtitlan, or at least the half of it that was dedicated to the Aztec god, was held to be a symbolic replication of this holy mountain.

Eventually, after more than a century of wandering without a settled homeland, the tribe found its way to the populous shores of Lake Texcoco. Here, sometime after AD1250, they settled on

A Gentler Age

If the Aztecs' idea of their own past mixed fact with legend, their view of their Toltec predecessors was still more deeply shrouded in a golden glow of myth.

The Aztecs supposed that in Toltec times the blood of animals was enough to quench the thirst of the gods.

"The Toltecs were wise, their works were all good, all perfect, all marvellous." So one native informant told the Spanish chronicler Father Bernardino de Sahagún, reflecting a general view of the splendours of the earlier civilization. The Toltecs were credited with inventing almost all the arts of civilization, from writing and goldworking to medicine.

Tollan, as the Aztecs called the Toltec capital, was described as a fabulous place where tropical birds abounded and cotton grew ready-dyed in multi-coloured hues. The descriptions were so glowing that for many years archaeologists failed to locate the city correctly, identifying it mistakenly with the ruins of

Teotihuacan, which had actually been destroyed a couple of hundred years before the Toltecs emerged into history.

It was only in the early 1940s that a Mexican historian found the real site. He did so by identifying place-names associated with it in Aztec sources with similarly named physical features surrounding the ruins at Tula in the state of Hidalgo, a hundred kilometres due north of Mexico City. His findings were rapidly accepted, and stimulated immediate archaeological interest in the previously little-explored site.

Discoveries made at Tula in the next five years confirmed its importance, while hardly justifying the encomia heaped on it by the Aztecs. In reality,

Tula's population was probably large by the standards of the day, but less than a third of the estimated 200,000 who had earlier crowded Teotihuacan. Then again, the markedly militaristic emphasis of the sculptures and reliefs found at Tula hardly squared with the Aztec vision of a nation of craftsman dedicated to the arts of peace.

The real roots of that imaginary Tollan seem to have lain not so much in memories of the city itself as in stories of its half-legendary ruler Topiltzin, who eventually became identified with the god Quetzalcoatl and encouraged his people to sacrifice serpents and butterflies in place of human (see pages 76–79).

Chapultepec, the Hill of the Locust, which is today the principal park of Mexico City. There they intermingled with other lakeside dwellers, many of them tribes who had completed a similar exodus in earlier years.

Chapultepec, however, turned out to be only a temporary refuge. The longer-established peoples took exception to their new neighbours, and formed a coalition to drive them away. The defeat was total: the Mexica ruler, known as Tlatoani or "He who Speaks", was captured and sacrificed. Reduced to beggary, the survivors had no option but to throw themselves on the mercy of their conquerors, who packed them off to the nearby region of Tizaapan, an unpopulated waste-land infested with snakes. Under the terms of their submission, the Mexica agreed to serve the rulers of Culhuacan as mercenary fighters, a task at which they soon proved their worth.

They also began to intermarry with their hosts, and were soon referring to themselves proudly as "Culhua-Mexica". This connection gave them particular satisfaction because Culhuacan had been settled by Toltec refugees after the decline of the city of Tula, and the link enabled them to claim descent from the creators of the last great pan-Mexican empire.

Unfortunately for the Mexica, the savagery of their customs soon brought this promising rela-tionship to an abrupt end. At the bidding of the priests of Huitzilopochtli, they approached the ruler of Culhuacan and asked for one of his daughters to be the bride of their god. Their over-lord graciously consented to the request. Sending the girl on ahead, he followed some days later to attend the festivities. He only realized the real meaning of the Mexica's petition when, peering through the gloom of Huitzilopochtli's shrine, he saw a priest wearing his daughter's skin, flayed from her body after she had been sacrificed to the god. Appalled, he called on his retinue of warriors to fall on her murderers and kill them.

In the ensuing fighting the Mexica were once again routed, this time taking refuge in the marshy fringes of Lake Texcoco itself. There at last, at the

A priest predicted that Tenochtitlan would be founded on the spot where an eagle was seen to perch on a cactus and eat a serpent, as depicted in this post-Conquest codex.

prompting of Huitzilopochtli, they finally found a permanent home. They ended up as they had started, inhabiting a lake island; but whereas Aztlan can never have been more than a rude tribal encampment, Tenochtitlan was to grow into one of the world's great cities.

99

The Conqueror God

When the Mexica were still wanderers in the wilderness, their tribal god Huitzilopochtli was a crucial part of their sense of national identity. In time he was to become an imperial deity, ever thirsty for fresh conquests – and for blood.

From the moment of his birth, Huitzilopochtli was a warrior god. As the Aztecs told the story, he was conceived miraculously by his mother Coatlicue, "She of the Serpent Skirt". This aged goddess was priestess of a mountaintop shrine at Coatepec, near Tula. One day, as she was sweeping out the sacred precinct, a ball of feathers fell from the sky. She placed it in her waistband and continued with her work, only to find when she looked for it later that it was gone. Soon after, the goddess discovered that she was pregnant, having been magically impregnated by the clump of down.

Pregnancy was far from a new experience for Coatlicue, as she already had a daughter, the moon goddess Coyolxauhqui, and no fewer than 400 sons; that figure – twenty times twenty – was often used by Mesoamericans to mean "innumerable". Her children were not expecting any further siblings, however, and when they noticed their mother's condition they reacted with furious indignation. Coatlicue, they imagined, had been guilty of sexual promiscuity, a grave sin in Mesoamerican eyes. At Coyolxauhqui's urging, they decided to kill her for her immorality.

The goddess and her 400 brothers assembled at the foot of Coatepec while their mother trembled in fear above. But the child she was carrying spoke to her from the womb, telling her not to fear. Sure enough, when his siblings launched their attack, Huitzilopochtli emerged from the womb armed and ready for battle. Startling though this notion might seem today, the idea was less so to the Aztecs themselves, who regarded new born male infants as warriors, while women who died in childbirth were considered to have been killed in battle with their own offspring. For all his precocious ferocity, the infant god could not save his mother, who was struck down and killed. But he made sure that she was amply avenged. First he cut down Coyolxauhqui, who had led the attack, cutting off her head and hurling her body down the mountainside, where it broke into pieces; "in various places her arms, her legs, her body each fell". Then he turned his attention to his brothers, killing them in their hundreds. Only a handful escaped to flee south.

"Hummingbird of the Left"

Huitzilopochtli was a relative newcomer to the Mesoamerican pantheon. Along with the other characters in the myth, he was among the very few deities to be introduced by the Mexica. While the Aztecs themselves explained Huitzilopochtli's leap to prominence by citing the myth of his birth, modern scholars have delved into Mexica legend in search of the god's real origins.

The name Huitzilopochtli means "Hummingbird of the Left" – "left" being a common synonym in the Nahuatl language for "south", the region with which the birds were associated. Although the tiny, brilliantly plumed creature might seem an odd symbol for such a sanguinary deity, it had long been associated with sacrificial blood-letting, compared metaphorically to a hummingbird sucking nectar from a flower.

Besides establishing Huitzilopochtli's might as a warrior, the story of his birth has been generally interpreted as a solar myth, with the newly born god routing his sisters and brothers just as the sun

Sacrificed bodies would tumble down the steps of the great pyramid at Tenochtitlan and land on this enormous stone carving of the moon goddess Coyolxauhqui's dismembered body.

100

Huitzilopochtli sacrifices his nephew and throws his heart into Lake Texcoco. The heart lands on a rocky islet – the very one where Tenochtitlan would later be built.

overwhelms the moon and stars at dawn. Yet in other aspects, the god had closer associations with fire. Although relatively few images of him survive, several that have show him wielding the Xiuhcoatl or fire serpent, a dragon-like creature that he purportedly used to strike down his siblings.

Above all Huitzilopochtli was a martial figure, displaying all the qualities of courage, vigour and authority that the Aztecs expected of their own rulers. That fact, together with his obvious tribal affiliations, has led some scholars to suggest that there may be a kernel of historical reality behind the legends. Some have proposed that, in certain aspects at least, the god may have been a mythologized reflection of an early leader of the Mexica, whose exploits were such that he was accorded divine status after his death.

The evidence for this view comes mostly from the story of the early wanderings. As the Aztecs told it, it was Huitzilopochtli himself who led the Mexica from Aztlan, their original home, and who instructed them to take up the bows, arrows and nets of nomad hunters. Promoters of the early-leader view have speculated that this story overlies a real historical episode.

Other historical events may be hidden behind later episodes of the saga. One account speaks of a factional dispute that led a group of the Mexica to break away under the leadership of Huitzilopochtli's sister, Malinalxochitl. This sibling gets no mention in the tale of the god's birth, a fact that in itself suggests that two cycles – one purely mythical and one partly historical – may have become confused. The secessionists found their way to a mountainous site some 70 kilometres southwest of the Valley of Mexico, later named Malinalco after their leader. There they established a settlement.

Relations between the two groups remained bad, and when Huitzilopochtli's followers eventually established themselves at Chapultepec on Lake Texcoco, it was Malinalxochitl's son, Copil, who led the neighbouring towns in arms against them. Although his troops won the day, Copil himself was captured and sacrificed by Huitzilopochtli, who cut out his heart and flung it into the middle of the lake. There it came to rest on an islet – the one, so legend asserted, on which the city of Tenochtitlan was later founded.

It was in his guise as tribal leader that Huitzilopochtli supposedly had a prophetic vision of the Aztecs' imperial destiny. According to the *Mexica Chronicle* of Hernando Alvarado Tezozomoc, published in about 1598, the god proclaimed: "We shall proceed to establish ourselves and settle down, and we shall conquer all peoples of the universe; and I tell you in all truth that I will make you lords and kings of all that is in the world; and when you become rulers, you shall have countless and infinite number of vassals, who will pay tribute to you." Although the pronouncement may have been concocted by propagandists during the glory days of empire, its attribution to

The Centre of the World

The Great Temple of Tenochtitlan was more than just a national shrine: it was the mid-point of the Aztec world.

Founded when the Aztecs settled in their capital, the Great Temple grew to become one of the biggest Mesoamerican shrines. The final version, completed in 1487, formed the centrepiece of a sacred precinct that included up to seventy-eight other buildings.

This area lay at the heart of Tenochtitlan, and was entered through gates oriented to the four directions. A fifth direction, that of the centre point, was marked by the temple itself. The vertical axis of the universe, made up of the layers of heaven and the Underworld, passed through it (see pages 58–59).

This codex from Central Mexico shows Xiuhtecuhtli at the centre of the universe from which the four directional World Trees emanate.

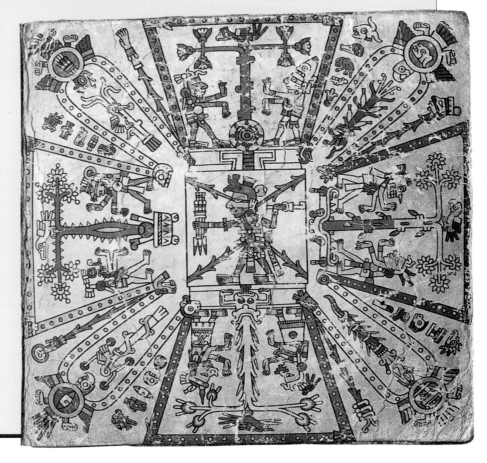

Huitzilopochtli nonetheless shows how he was linked with expansion and conquest.

Like much of the commentary on Meso-american religion, such speculations are almost impossible to prove or disprove. What is certain is that whatever historical facts went into the creation of the god were soon overlaid with a thick patina of myth. As the supreme deity of an imperial power, Huitzilopochtli needed to be assigned a suitably august place in the celestial hierarchy. The priests quickly identified him with Tezcatlipoca, at the time the most powerful figure in the Mesoamerican pantheon; the two were referred to as brothers, and in ritual were often jointly honoured. Each played an important role in the annual festivals asso-ciated with the other; and in the cere-monies preceding a new ruler's assump-tion of power, the future king invoked the older god while standing before Huitzilopochtli's shrine.

A Link with the Rain God

Another divine connection that helped lend authority to the new god was with the rain god Tlaloc, the most ancient and time-honoured of all Mesoamerican divinities. The twin shrines to the two deities on the summit of the Great Temple at Tenochtitlan made the link clear, and also symbolized the coming together of "fire and water" – a phrase the Aztecs used, because of the irreconcilable nature of the two elements, as a synonym for war. Although the majority of sacrifices at the temple were dedicated to Huitzilopochtli, archaeological investigation has revealed many more images of Tlaloc among its remains, perhaps indicating greater popular enthu-siasm for the older god.

But in public life at least, Huitzilopochtli was unchallenged in his role as national deity. The greatest festival of the ceremonial year was Panquetzaliztli, which was dedicated to him. The

Huitzilopochtli's lieutenant, Ixtilton, visited children in their sleep and brought them darkness and rest. This obsidian mask of his face was made just before the Conquest.

104

festival's name meant "Raising of the Banners", for it was celebrated at a time when the harvest was in and the nation was preparing for the season devoted to warfare – an apt time to invoke the nation's divine warlord. Songs were composed in the god's honour and men and women danced together in the forecourts of the temples.

The festival was marked by more than the usual number of human sacrifices. Most were prisoners of war offered up by the warriors who had taken them captive. But merchants – another pillar of the Aztec state – were also given the chance to glorify Huitzilopochtli through the donation of so-called "bathed slaves". Few customs so well illustrate the brutal nature of Aztec society, which allowed wealthy traders to gain status and to participate in some of the privileges of the warrior aristocracy at the cost of other people's lives.

Preparations for the sacrifice began months in advance, when a merchant eager to improve his professional standing would purchase four attractive male or female slaves, preferably with a talent for singing or dancing. The buyer would then embark on a period of conspicuous expenditure, building houses, giving expensive presents to the elders of his own profession and to influential nobles, and setting off on pilgrimage to Tochtepec, a central entrepot on the trade route to the southern lands, where he would entertain the mercantile community based in the town.

Meanwhile the slaves, who were well treated, were expected to earn their keep by entertaining guests at the lavish feasts the merchant hosted for much of the year. Then, nine days before the start of Panquetzaliztli, the slaves were bathed with water from a spring sacred to the god. A round of religious ceremonies began that culminated on the final day of the festival.

On that day the slaves, in the presence of the Aztec emperor and a huge crowd of onlookers, were led four times round the Great Temple in Tenochtitlan. They and their master then climbed the stairs that led to Huitzilopochtli's shrine on the pyramid's summit. At the top, the merchant consigned his purchases to the waiting priests, who stretched the slaves across the sacrificial stone and cut out their hearts as offerings to the god.

The bodies were subsequently returned to their owner, who took them home to serve as the centrepiece of a ritual banquet. Stewed and served on a bed of maize, the flesh was offered to all the merchants' kinsmen, who had been solemnly invited to join him in celebrating his elevation into the upper ranks of the mercantile class.

In the case of bathed slaves as for prisoners of war, Huitzilopochtli's acceptance of the offerings was a mark of divine approval that confirmed and enhanced the status of the giver. As the supreme god of the Aztec state, he guaranteed the integrity of the prevailing social order just as he did the authority of the empire.

To what extent Huitzilopochtli commanded the loyalty, rather than simply the respect, of the mass of the population, is harder to tell, but the relative ease with which Cortés and his successors erased his traces after the conquest suggests that, even among the Aztecs themselves, he was more feared than loved.

A merchant and his friends and family share a meal of the remains of one of their slaves with the god of death, Mictlantecuhtli, in a detail from a 15th-century codex.

Rebirth of the Sun

From earlier cultures the Aztecs inherited a fascination with the sky, seen as the realm of the gods. In the night, cosmic dramas were played out in the heavens that only the initiated could ever hope to understand.

Sometime shortly before the arrival of Cortés on the Mexican coast, the emperor Motecuhzoma II had a vision. In his palace he saw a great grey bird with a black mirror mounted on its forehead. He immediately recognized this as the magical divining glass of the god Tezcatlipoca in which the mysteries of the universe were revealed.

Looking into its depths, he saw the night sky and all its stars, a view he knew well for he was a trained observer of the heavens. Suddenly the scene changed, and in its place he made out the image of oddly dressed warriors armed with unfamiliar weapons. They stared at him menacingly, and he instinctively knew that they represented a terrible threat to himself and to his kingdom.

Aztec informants told this tale to the Spanish chronicler Bernardino de Sahagún after the Conquest, and it may well have been embroidered with the benefit of hindsight. It is also likely that the emperor, at the time when he had his premonition, had heard reports of an earlier Spanish expedition that had coasted the continent.

What is not in dispute, however, is that no-one was surprised that the emperor should have seen such an apparition, nor that the heavens should have featured in it. For the Aztec emperor was a semi-divine being who could expect to receive messages from the gods; and the night sky was where he most often looked to find them.

Astronomy played a central role in the intellectual life of all Mesoamerican cultures; no subject, with the possible exception of mathematics, was so closely studied. The institution through which knowledge of the heavens was passed down seems to have been the *calmecac*, the religious schools where the sons of the nobility were educated and new priests trained.

Motecuhzoma II was imprisoned and then murdered by Cortés in 1521. This detail from Bernardino de Sahagún's chronicle shows him dreaming of his own death.

The Maya – the most assiduous of Mesoamerican stargazers – are thought to have built observatories. An unusual circular building at Chichen Itza known from its shape as the *Caracol*, or "Snail", was one such, its upper-storey windows apparently positioned to command views of the various phases of Venus. The movements of this planet, whose influence was considered to be malign, were of considerable interest to Mayan rulers, who are known to have timed military assaults to coincide with its rising.

Throughout Mesoamerica, astronomy was pursued not so much for its own sake as to learn what the stars presaged for life on Earth; in this respect, its study came closer to astrology than to the modern science. So in Motecuhzoma's time it was a duty of the Aztec emperor to scan the heavens three times daily, at sunrise, sunset and midnight, for signs that might indicate good or evil fortune. The position of the planets, the sudden appearance of meteorites (a good omen), unusual displays of light or oddly shaped clouds were all noted and analysed for their significance.

Yet it was not just the future that the heavens could reveal. The sky was also a stage on which the great cosmic myths might be replayed. Most of the major gods had their stellar counterparts; for example, Tezcatlipoca was identified with the

Rending the Earth Monster

Part of the Aztecs' legacy from central Mexico was an ancient myth that told how the world and the sky were created from the body of the Earth Monster Tlaltecuhtli, a fearsome ogress who would only let crops flourish if she was fed with human blood.

A Totonac stela of the Earth Monster from c.1250 shows her feeding on a sacrificial human heart.

Tlaltecuhtli's taste for flesh was so great that a single gaping maw toothed with flint knives was not enough to satisfy her bestial appetites; she had subsidiary mouths at her elbows, knees and other joints that also gnashed hungrily. She looked so fearsome that even the other gods were in awe of her. Eventually Tezcatlipoca and Quetzalcoatl, putting aside their usual differences, decided to rid the world of her so as to permit the process of creation to get under way.

Transforming themselves into giant serpents, they grappled with Tlaltecuhtli, finally managing to tear her huge body in two. (In another version of the story, Tezcatlipoca fought in his own guise and lost a foot in the struggle.) Then they threw one half of the corpse up into the sky, where it was transformed into the vault of the heavens.

Meanwhile other gods, shocked by the violence done to Tlaltecuhtli despite all the havoc she had wreaked, determined to form the Earth from the other half of her body. They made trees, flowers and herbs spring from her hair; wells and springs were fashioned from her eyes; her mouth served for rivers and caverns; and from her nose rose mountain ranges and valleys.

So life returned to the recumbent goddess, and with it much of her old ferocity. For sometimes in the night she could be heard screaming for human blood and hearts – the only diet that could persuade her to continue to bring forth nature's bounty.

Great Bear, and Aztec astronomers saw a commemoration of the time when he lost a foot in battle with the Earth Monster in the constellation's descent into the sea. Xolotl, who accompanied Quetzalcoatl to the Underworld (see pages 128–129), was Venus as the Evening Star.

The realm of gods and portents, the sky was regarded with profound awe as a sacred precinct quite beyond the reach of humankind. On Earth, those places that approached closest to it, such as mountain-tops and temple-pyramids, were regarded with special veneration.

A similar dichotomy to the one splitting earth from sky separated day and night. The first belonged to mundane reality and the human

The sinister deity Xolotl, Quetzalcoatl's evil twin, represented Venus as the Evening Star. In this Aztec pottery image, he wears the star on his forehead.

sphere; but the hours of darkness were a threatening interval when supernatural forces were in the ascendant. Between sunset and sunrise, demons and shape-shifters walked abroad, and fearsome ghosts might rise up from the Underworld to haunt the living. Sleep was also regarded as a dangerous activity in which the soul left the slumbering body, sometimes to travel great distances.

On its journeys the soul risked perilous encounters with ancestors, gods and other unearthly beings; these confrontations might subsequently be recollected in the form of dreams. Dreams could also contain prophetic insights; so when Cortés first landed in Aztec territory, Motecuhzoma decreed that the citizens of Tenochtitlan should report unusual visions that had come to them as they slept, and was rewarded with ominous accounts of the city's temples fallen and palaces destroyed.

Demons of the Night

The most fearsome of all the supernatural beings that haunted the night were the *tzitzimime*, malevolent female spirits transformed into stars who kept baleful watch on the human world below them. They bore a grudge against the living, and were held responsible for many ills, including injuries and disease; as such, they took the blame for the various epidemics that decimated the population after the Spanish Conquest.

At particularly unpropitious times – notably, the end of each fifty-two-year cycle of the Aztec calendar (see pages 116–117) – it was thought that they turned back into vengeful demons who could launch themselves like arrows from the heavens to fall upon the earth in search of victims. Their coming was feared all the more because in the long run it was expected to bring cosmic disaster. It was they who would ultimately destroy the Fifth Sun and bring human life to an end.

One period when their influence was especially strong was during solar eclipses. These phenomena were regarded with particular alarm as a time when the night and its supernatural horrors

Lord of the Dawn

When the Mesoamericans looked at the heavens, they saw signs of cosmic conflict, not divine order. For them, the dawn was not so much serene as blood-stained, and its Lord was a mighty warrior whose anger was terrible.

For the Aztecs and their neighbours, Tlahuizcal-pantecuhtli – an aspect of Quetzalcoatl – was the Morning Star, the planet Venus when it appears before sunrise. This was an inauspicious time, and its presiding spirit was feared as a fierce deity whose anger could be terrible.

Priests charted the course of Venus carefully, and drew up almanacs showing likely targets for the god's wrath. Sometimes these were whole categories of people, such as infants or the old; at other periods, however, his resentment might be turned against the rain, in which case drought could be expected to follow. People took these warnings seriously, blocking up doors and windows at times when they thought they were at risk from Venus's malignant rays.

The Morning Star, a fearsome creature, throws his rays at the Earth in the form of darts.

encroached menacingly on the day. Individuals with fair complexions were sacrificed to fortify the sun, and a wave of penitential blood-letting swept across the land as individuals perforated their bodies in the hope of keeping the *tzitzimime* at bay.

Another time of tension was the dawn, when day and night met again and the sun was reborn from the Underworld. According to one tradition, it was pulled up to its zenith by the souls of warriors slain in battle; on its downward journey later in the day, its companions were the *cilhuateteo*, women who had died in childbirth.

Different deities were associated with the sun in its day and night-time phases. When it travelled through the Underworld in the hours of darkness, it took the form of Tepeyollotl, the "Heart of the Mountains", a jaguar whose roar could be heard in the sound of avalanches and volcanic eruptions. By day it was Tonatiuh, a weapon-wielding soldier who became the centre of a militaristic cult; soldiers were encouraged to face death fearlessly in the knowledge that, if they were killed in combat, they would enjoy a happy afterlife in his train.

Yet the moment of transition just before sunrise was always a dangerous one, for it was never entirely certain that Tonatiuh would consent to embark on his journey. For the Aztecs, racked by cosmic insecurity, harked back always to the story of the creation of the Fifth Sun (see pages 84–85), when the god had stood still.

109

TEOTIHUACAN

Teotihuacan was the great metropolis of the Classic era, and in its heyday around AD500 was one of the world's biggest cities. Orderly residential neighbourhoods crowded with tenement blocks stretched away from a central ceremonial artery, which became known to later peoples as the Avenue of the Dead. There, temples and palaces flanked an imposing sequence of open spaces and plazas culminating in the sixty-metre-high Pyramid of the Moon.

Right: The Pyramid of the Moon was shorter than the Pyramid of the Sun, but it was built on higher ground so the summits of the two structures were level.

Far right: A carved serpent's head from the Temple of Quetzalcoatl typifies the florid decorative touches that enhanced many of the city's monuments.

Above: A mask from a burial cache illustrates the serenity of Teotihuacan art, with its taste for what have been called "clear, anonymous faces, neither male nor female, young nor old".

Above: Seen from the top of the Pyramid of the Moon, the ruins of Teotihuacan stretch into the distance along the Avenue of the Dead. To the left, the Pyramid of the Sun – Mesoamerica's largest ruin – rises 65m above the surrounding plain.

Right: The most pervasive feature of Teotihuacan architecture in the so-called *talud-tablero* profile of the facades of the major buildings. This consists of a vertical rectangular face *(tablero)* and a sloping one *(talud)* which alternate with each other

RITUAL AND BELIEF

Mythology was very much a part of daily life in Mesoamerica. Recorded in stone and in paint, the deeds of the gods were regularly re-enacted in public ceremonies that were rich in pomp, pageantry and theatrical flair. The very architecture of the temples provided elevated stages for the enactment of ritual dramas. And in the streets of the cities, a constant round of festivals ensured that the gods were never far from people's minds.

Yet underpinning all the ceremonial activity were highly abstruse and esoteric calculations. One aspect was a fascination with numerology and an obsession with auspicious and inauspicious days. Most Mesoamerican peoples were accustomed to operating two separate calendars – the familiar one of 365-day and another, 260-day round that was handed down specifically for the purpose of augury. Some also calculated the passing of time in lengthy year-cycles, akin to our centuries, the conception of which demanded a firm sense of history; in the case of the Maya Long Count, the periods involved stretched over many thousands of years.

Below: **The pyramid temple at Uxmal, built around AD800, is a classic example of the power of Mesoamerican temple architecture.**

In marked contrast to the cerebral side of the region's religion was its brutal emphasis on sacrifice, commonly of human beings. The notion of placating capricious and often cruel deities by offering up something precious was fundamental to all the region's faiths – and blood was generally taken to be the greatest gift of all. But victims were sometimes seen as more than just offerings. They could be messengers to the gods, or even their temporary personifications. Another channel of communication to the divine

lay through shamanistic trance, often brought on by the use of hallucinogens. An ancient practice thought to have come from Siberia, shamanism was common among all the native peoples of America.

At the end of all peoples' strivings was death, and here Mesoamerican religion had little comfort to offer. The gods had to be appeased to obtain favours and to prevent catastrophes befalling the living, and people with special powers could be consulted to try to guess their will. But they had no concern with morality, and provided no promise of salvation in the afterlife. As a result, the world people faced after death was like the one they knew in life, a dangerous and threatening place, offering little more than the prospect of impending perils followed by the final likelihood of extinction.

Opposite: **This sacrificial deer has been turned into a decorative motif in a Mexican codex. Animal sacrifice was common among Mesoamerican peoples, but beasts were considered a poor substitute for humans.**

Cycles of Destiny

The dangerous gods of Mesoamerica were the masters of time, dictating the fates of hapless humans according to capricious whim. In order to attempt to predict the next move in the gods' game of life and death, priests developed a complex system of two calendars.

The 3-metre-wide Calendar Stone, found in Mexico City in the 18th century, depicts the 260-day annual cycle. Its size and magnificence show how significant the keeping of time was to the Aztecs. Glyphs of the twenty day signs surround the Earth Monster. The four panels represent the four worlds previously destroyed by the gods.

roughly 365 and a quarter days. So they had no equivalent to the leap year, introduced into European calendrics by Julius Caesar in 46BC.

The result was that over time the Meso-american solar year wandered through the seasons. To keep any kind of agricultural relevance, it must have been corrected from time to time, though such amendments have gone unrecorded. Because of its imprecision, archaeologists refer to it as the Vague Year. Yet it had huge significance as the main measure of time for public events.

From early on, the Mesoamericans had a solar year of 365 days, which they split into twenty 18-day months, each one reflecting the influence of a particular deity and including a festival in his or her honour (see pages 138–139). In the Aztec calendar, gods associated with the cultivation of maize predominated in the earlier part of the year, when agricultural activity was busiest. Later came festivals for warriors, hunters and women. The year ended with five so-called "nameless" days, necessary to round off the 365. As these were under the protection of no particular god, they were considered ill-omened, and people avoided undertaking any major enterprise at this time.

The calendar was imperfect, however, for Mesoamerican mathematics lacked fractions, and so never came to terms with the fact that the actual length of the Earth's revolution around the sun is

The 260-day Calendar

Alongside the 365-day calendar, another of equal significance and possibly even greater antiquity was regularly consulted. This was a 260-day almanac, in which each day bore a number from one to thirteen and one of twenty names – for example, Wind, Dog or Deer – which, like the numbers, rotated in a fixed order. So, in the Aztec version, the day named One Caiman was followed by Two Wind and Three House; once Thirteen Reed had been reached, the sequence continued with One Jaguar (Jaguar being fourteenth in the day-name sequence). One Caiman was reached again on the 261st day of this never-ending cycle.

Unlike the solar calendar, the 260-day count had no apparent link with the seasons or the movements of heavenly bodies, which has led to much debate about how it originally came into use. A likely explanation is that it was devised by midwives as an aid to calculating the gestation of babies, from the time of the mother's first missed period to the birth. The facts that individuals in many parts of Central America took their names from their birthday as measured by the count and were reckoned at that time to have already completed one 260-day cycle – in effect, to have been born on their first birthday – point in that direction.

The origins of the 260-day calendar remain obscure, but the evidence suggests that it was in use in much of Mesoamerica by the first century AD. It played a central role in Maya life in the Classic era just as it was to do in Aztec times a thousand years later; in fact, many day-names were shared by the two cultures.

While the 365-day calendar served to measure the passing seasons, the 260-day cycle was primarily a guide to the future, providing a crucial tool for diviners to foretell private fortunes as well as the likely outcome of affairs of state. Every day reflected the influence of gods and other forces

Even though they were associated with death and the night, owls were also linked with the Lords of the Day.

that could be propitious or unpropitious. Firstly, the thirteen numbers of the sequence each had their divine patrons, the so-called Lords of the Day, who were associated with the thirteen levels of the heavens and with a similar number of flying creatures – hummingbirds, owls, butterflies, doves. Secondly, each of the twenty day-names came

A Living Tradition

Despite the advent of Christianity, some Mesoamerican beliefs have survived to the present day. In particular, the ritual 260-day calendar is still alive among highland Maya communities.

Among the Ixil, Quiché and other peoples of Guatemala and southern Mexico, shaman priests known as day-keepers still reckon the passing of time by the twenty signs and thirteen numbers of the Maya. Villagers turn to these community healers for reading omens, protection against ill health and advice on their future projects.

One of the biggest communal celebrations geared to the old calendar is the Eight Monkey Festival in the Quiché community of Momostenango in Guatemala. The festival is still held on that date of the 260-day year. Although nominally Christian, the feast clearly encompasses memories of the old faith.

On the appointed day tens of thousands of Indians gather at first light in company with a hundred or more shamans. They come to honour the god they call Dios Mundo (God of the Earth), praying for past forgiveness and future blessing around piles of broken pottery that serve as altars. To speed each prayer on its way, fresh shards are added to the piles – a distant echo of the human or animal sacrifices that in past times would have accompanied similar appeals to the gods.

under the sway of a specific deity. And thirdly, the forces prevailing at the start of each thirteen-day period cast a lingering spell over the remaining twelve days. The result was a rich stew of associations that could be interpreted only by trained priests. Even so, some days were so obviously bad that children born on them were sometimes renamed on more auspicious ones.

The Aztecs called the 260-day cycle the *tonalpohualli* – literally, "counting of the day-signs" – and had a myth to describe how it had come into being. The first humans, they claimed, had felt the need for such a calendar and had taken their concerns to the oldest of all the gods, the divine couple Cipactonal and Oxomoco. Oxomoco chose a symbol for the first day. She selected the caiman, after which the other nineteen day-signs fell into place of their own accord. The first almanac of all the signs was then drawn up, and their grandson Quetzalcoatl passed the art of divining from it down to humankind.

The lessons that could be learned from a proper reading of the calendar were vast indeed. According to the chronicler Fra Diego Duran, the *tonalpohualli* "taught the Indian nations the days

on which they were to sow, reap, till the land, cultivate corn, weed, harvest, store, shell the ears of corn, sow beans and flax seed." It was equally indispensable to merchants setting out on expeditions or rulers contemplating policy decisions.

If 260 days had to pass before a given number and name – Twelve Reed, say – came round again on this cycle, a much longer period had to elapse before a Twelve Reed day coincided with a particular date in the 365-day year. Mesoamerican mathematicians worked out that it took a total of 18,980 days for the two year-counts to mesh – a period equivalent to fifty-two 365-day years and seventy-three revolutions of the 260-day cycle. This mathematical fact attained huge importance for various Mesoamerican peoples, for whom the Calendar Round – the name modern historians have given the fifty-two-year period – took on great mystical significance. The Aztecs referred to it as "the bundle of years", from the custom of storing a peeled stick to mark the passage of each

Each day in the 260-day calendar was associated with a particular god or myth, as this colourful detail in the pre-Conquest *Codex Cospi* shows.

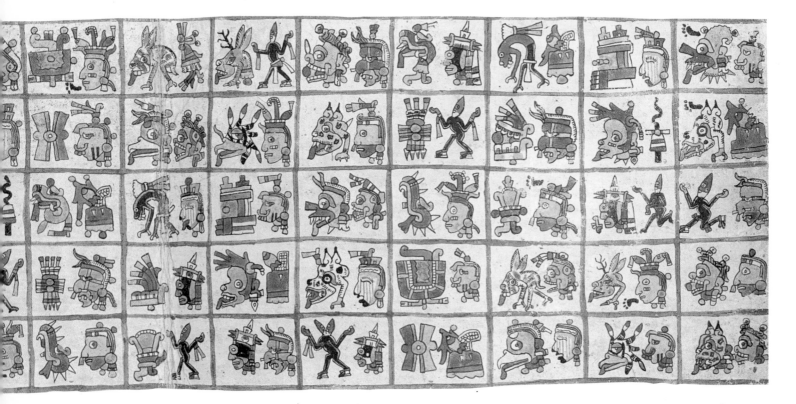

At the end of every 52-year cycle, people all over the Valley of Mexico waited on rooftops to see the sacred flame lit near Tenochtitlan. Then a courier carried the flame from house to house for the people to light their own fires.

solar year; the wands were then tied into a faggot and ritually burned once fifty-two had been collected. They awaited the moment with trepidation, for they believed that in a very real sense it represented the end of time, the moment when the gods might choose to destroy the world. As the fateful time approached, people shattered their household utensils, let their fires go out, abstained from sex, fasted, kept silence, and gradually abandoned all their daily activities.

On the night itself, a solemn procession passed out of the capital, headed for an ancient shrine on a nearby peak. There the assembled priests and dignitaries waited in utter silence until midnight, carefully watching the Pleiades. If this star cluster continued to move after it had reached its zenith, it was taken as a signal that the world was not about to end.

To celebrate the survival of the world, priests sacrificed an important victim – usually a captured prince or general – by cutting out his heart on an altar on the mountain top. A priest would then strike fire on a fire-drill within the cavity where the victim's heart had been. When the sparks had strengthened into a flame, they were used to ignite a great bonfire.

Then, people who had been waiting anxiously on their rooftops would raise a cheer at this confirmation that the end was not at hand. Subsequently the flame was carried to the Great Temple in Tenochtitlan itself. After months of tension, people could at last relax; their world was safe – at least for another fifty-two years.

117

A Universe Fuelled by Blood

The gods had set the world in motion and, through their magical calendar, had determined the fate of those who lived in it. They expected something in return from their creation – and the most valuable gift of all was blood.

To modern eyes, the most startling aspect of the Mesoamerican world was its emphasis on sacrifice and blood, yet to the people of the time the need for such offerings would have seemed self-evident. For the region's gods were not benevolent. They were as capricious as they were all-powerful, and human beings only survived on sufferance. Both the Mayas and the Aztecs believed that in past aeons the gods had created and then destroyed several worlds. The world they lived in would only survive if people did all in their power to avert the anger of the gods. There were several mechanisms by which the gods could be appeased. Due care and attention was one

A captive is prepared for sacrifice with his arms tied behind his back and an incision above his heart in this Totonac carving from between AD500 and 900.

such a method. According to the Maya chronicle the *Popul Vuh*, one earlier race of people had already been destroyed for failing to praise the gods. Subsequent generations took care never to repeat the mistake.

Images of the leading deities were carefully tended in their shrines, and were regularly paraded before the people at festivals. Offerings of all kinds were made to them, not just at the temples but also in sacred places including caves and mountaintop shrines. A whole cache of treasures, including food containers and artworks from conquered lands, was buried in the foundations of the Aztecs' Great Temple of Tenochtitlan, while the Sacred Cenote, or sink-hole, at Chichen Itza (see pages 80–81) has yielded up many valuables, including gold discs and ornaments of jade.

More Precious Than Gold

Ultimately, however, the gods sought something more precious to them than gold, and that was blood. The blood of animals was an acceptable offering, and in Aztec times quails were slaughtered in large numbers, their heads torn off before the sacred images. Dogs and turkeys were also frequent victims, and on important occasions jaguars were sometimes killed; sixteen died to celebrate the accession of the sixteenth ruler of Copan, and a jaguar skeleton was uncovered in the Tenochtitlan temple foundations.

For the most part, though, human blood was the offering the gods most desired. The *Popol Vuh* recounts how Tohil, patron deity of the Quiché Maya, specifically rejected offerings of precious metal in favour of flesh. By Aztec times, the demand for victims had become so great that special wars were fought in which the aim was not to kill the enemy but to take captives who would subsequently end up on sacrificial altars.

Though evidence for earlier periods is slight, it seems likely that human sacrifice on a smaller scale went far back in the history of the area. But the quantity of killing seems to have increased greatly with the ending of the so-called Classic Age in the seventh or eighth century AD. By Toltec times, skull-racks for displaying heads of victims became a common feature of ceremonial centres. At Tenochtitlan, a huge skull-rack stood between the Great Temple and the ball court.

Though most victims were prisoners-of-war or slaves, individuals of all ranks were also expected to contribute their own blood through the practice known as auto-sacrifice. This involved passing sharp implements – thorn-studded twine, stingray spines, spikes from the maguey plant – through fleshy parts of the body, including the earlobes, cheeks, lips, tongue and foreskin. The blood was then usually smeared on to paper and burned before statues of the gods.

The Origins of Human Sacrifice

Mythology provided explanations for these sanguinary obsessions. One Aztec myth described how the present world was created when Quetzalcoatl and Tezcatlipoca tore the Earth Monster Tlaltecuhtli in two, transforming one half of her torso into the sky and the other into the earth (see page 107). All growing things were fashioned from her body. At night, it was said, she could sometimes be heard howling for the hearts of men to eat, and her hunger had to be satisfied if she was to continue to provide nature's bounty.

Another story told how two gods sacrificed themselves to become the Sun and Moon. Both rose into the sky, but remained there motionless.

A priest slaughters a captive in honour of the gods in this stela from Guatemala. Human sacrifice was an important part of Mesoamerican culture from the earliest civilizations.

119

It was common for victims to be sacrificed at the top of the temple steps. When the heart had been removed, the body was flung to the ground. Eyewitnesses described the steps streaming with blood. This graphic illustration is from the *Codex Magliabechiano*, which was painted by Aztec artists under the direction of Spanish friars soon after the Conquest.

The sun god, Tonatiuh, declared that he would not move unless the other deities gave him their own blood as a sign of fealty. When the other gods agreed to have their hearts cut out, he began his journey. Ever after, humans had to repeat the gods' gesture if Tonatiuh was to continue his passage through the heavens.

In practice sacrifice also served other, more practical purposes in Aztec society. The great majority of victims were prisoners-of-war, and the demands of the sacrificial altars provided a justification and a rationale for constant military activity. This in turn served the interests of the ruling warrior class, whose position at the peak of the social hierarchy rested on battlefield prowess.

If any one person's hand can be seen behind the upsurge in killing that marked the Aztec heyday, it was probably that of a nobleman called Tlacaelel, who served as adviser to three successive rulers in the fifteenth century. According to the Dominican chronicler Diego Durán, who drew his information from Aztec sources soon after the Conquest, Tlacaelel was not merely a great general, "bold and cunning in the trickery of war", but he also "invented devilish, cruel and frightful sacrifices". For although detailed figures are hard to

estimate, there seems to have been a quantum leap in the number of sacrificial victims under the Aztecs in the latter part of the fifteenth century.

Ritual killings formed part of most, if not all, of the festivals that marked the twenty months of the agricultural year. Special events could call for the sacrifice of thousands. The rededication of the Great Temple of Tenochtitlan in 1487 was said to have been marked by the mass slaughter of 20,000 or even as many as 80,000 victims.

The most common form of sacrifice in Aztec times was the cutting out of hearts. Four priests would hold the victim spreadeagled over a sacrificial altar while a fifth, equipped with a razor-sharp flint knife, would rapidly cut out the heart. The hearts themselves – still pulsating – were raised up towards the sun by the officiating priest. Then the blood-soaked body bumped slowly down the steps of the pyramid to land in a sodden heap at its base. Old men collected the bodies for dismemberment. Skulls were displayed on the skull-rack in the temple compound.

Bernal Diaz, one of the conquistadors who accompanied Cortés, wrote an account of his visit to the Great Temple of Tenochtitlan: "There were some smoking braziers of their incense, which they call copal, in which they were burning the hearts of three Indians whom they had sacrificed that day; and all the walls of that shrine were so splashed and caked with blood that they and the floor too were black ... The stench was worse than that of any slaughterhouse in Spain."

The bodies of prisoners-of-war were retrieved afterwards by their captors, and parts of them were consumed by members of their families in ritual feasts. These cannibal meals were solemn affairs, for the flesh of the victims was considered to be consecrated and was, in the words of one chronicler, "eaten with reverence, ritual and fastidiousness – as if it were something from Heaven". As a gesture of humility, the warrior himself would refrain from eating in case he himself should end up in a similar situation at some future date.

Other forms of sacrifice, including beheading and shooting with darts, were also practised in the course of the monthly festivals, in which the victims were for the most part considered representatives of the gods (see pages 122–123). Those to be killed were treated with respect by their captors, and were promised a happy afterlife in the upper levels of the Aztec Heaven.

Yet few free-born citizens ever volunteered for the honour. Death on the altars was almost invariably imposed by the powerful on the weakest members of society. The great mass of the population apparently stoically accepted human sacrifice as an institution that was sanctioned by both age-old custom and the divine order.

Rites of Confession

The sense of sin weighed heavily on several of the Mesoamerican peoples. To lessen the burden, they had recourse to self-mortification and to rituals of confession.

Post-Conquest accounts describe penitential rituals among the Zapotec and Maya. Zapotecs would pierce their flesh and allow the blood to drip onto maize husks as they recounted their transgressions. Certain Maya communities chose a scapegoat – usually an old woman – to bear the sins of the whole community. After hearing the confessions of each individual, the victim would be stoned to death, thereby winning atonement for the entire village.

The best-attested rites are those of the pre-Conquest Aztecs. Deeply puritanical in their attitude towards sex, they felt the need to purify themselves

ritually of the stain it cast upon them. Men were given a single chance to do so by a once-in-a-lifetime confession to the goddess Tlazolteotl.

At a time of his choosing, usually in late middle age, the penitent would strip naked and confess his misdemeanours to a priest representing the goddess. He would then be offered absolution, but not before he had been forced to carry out a series of painful penances.

A Maya ballplayer is dressed in the simple clothes of a penitent. His bruised and swollen face drips with blood from a bloodletting ritual.

Impersonating the Gods

The concept that someone could become divine by dressing up in the regalia of the gods was an ancient one in Mesoamerica, and it was to provide the Aztecs with a rationale for some of their most bizarre and harrowing rituals.

Virtually all Mesoamerican peoples were used to seeing representations of the gods in pottery and stone. Given the theatrical nature of much of their public ritual, it was then a natural step to incorporate living images of the deities into festivals and other ceremonies in the form of humans splendidly adorned in their vestments traditionally associated with individual divinities.

For participants and spectators alike, the concept went far beyond any idea of play-acting. When Maya kings put on costumes that reproduced the traditional outfits of the Maize God or the Jaguar God of the Underworld, they were thought to become temporarily divine themselves.

Under the Aztecs, the concept became linked with the cult of human sacrifice. In an extension of previous practice, victims known as *ixiptla* were dressed up, each as a particular god. Treated with the respect due to the divinity they were held to

have become, they were then sacrificed to that same deity. All the gods of the twenty Aztec months seem to have been celebrated in this way. But the concept of divine impersonation was expressed in its most extreme form in the shape of the young man – handsome, smooth-skinned and intelligent – chosen to represent Tezcatlipoca every year at the end of the month dedicated to the deity. For a whole year he was honoured as the living representative of the god.

During the day he was kept under guard in Tezcatlipoca's temple, where he was trained to dance and play the flute. At night he was released in the company of eight young warriors, who acted both as his attendants and as sentinels to check that he did not escape. As he walked through the deserted night-time streets, he played on his flute and rattled bangles attached to his arms and legs. Citizens who heard the sounds told

Sacred Bundles

One feature that Mesoamerican religion shared with some native faiths of North America was the veneration of bundles containing objects sacred to the cult of a particular god.

Examples of sacred bundles have been found in Maya artwork of the Classic period, and the *Popol Vuh* recounts how the Quiché Maya carried one such pack representing an ancestor with them on their migrations. Chichemec peoples including the Mixtecs and Aztecs adopted

the practice, which had obvious attractions for nomads forced to take their gods with them on their travels.

Aztec bundles purportedly included the gods' mantles, bequeathed to retainers in the legendary past when they had sacrificed themselves to bring

life to the world; to these were added jade, jewels, snake and jaguar skins and other holy objects. The relics were entrusted to priests known as "god-bearers", who acquired special powers from them including the ability to pronounce oracles.

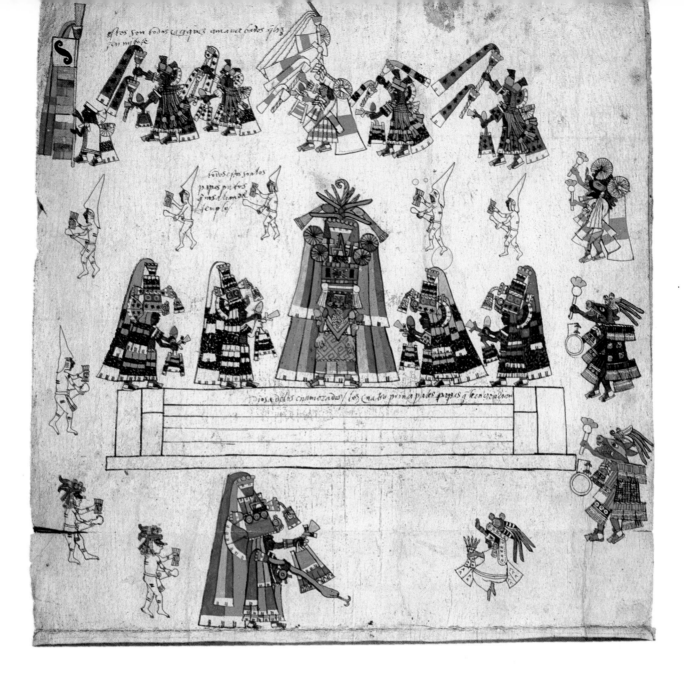

each other that the god himself was passing; some would bring out sick children for his blessing, hoping to see them cured.

The adulation rose to a climax as the month sacred to Tezcatlipoca came round again. In those final twenty days the Aztec ruler himself came to the temple to dress the youth in the full regalia of the god. He was provided with four wives, themselves held to represent important goddesses. Five days before the end of the month, the emperor went into temporary retreat to indicate that the living Tezcatlipoca reigned supreme in the city. When the final day came, the youth was taken to

A priest in the striped headdress of the maize goddess and flanked by other priests dressed as the rain god's assistants performs a ritual in a detail from a 16th-century Aztec codex.

the shrine of the god, where he bade his wives farewell. Then he mounted the pyramid. When he reached the top, he was sacrificed. The dead body was carried down to ground level, where it was butchered. The flesh was later cooked in a stew served to the ruler and other dignitaries at a banquet. One of the guests was the youth who had earlier in the day been selected to be the god's new representative – and next year's main course.

123

The Power of the Shaman

Mesoamerican religion may have had its roots in shamanistic rites imported across the Bering land bridge from Asia. Their influence was long lasting: shape-shifting sorcerers were feared long after the Conquest and spirit journeys are still part of popular myth.

The ability to enter trances, to fly supernaturally, and to cure spirits, plus the possession of animal spirit companions, are all features of the shaman. Hallucinogens that were known to later peoples, including narcotic mushrooms, morning-glory seeds and peyote, may also have been used to induce trances and visions from an early time.

By Aztec times, different terms were used to describe the two aspects of the shamanistic relationship between man and beast. In the Nahuatl language, *tonal* served to describe the animal familiar spirits associated with most individuals from shortly after their birth.

The technique of shape-shifting and the sorcerers who had learned its secrets were both denoted by the word *nahual*. Such individuals were greatly feared, as was their patron deity, the mighty but sinister Tezcatlipoca. While many Aztec divinities had the ability to transform themselves, he was particularly noted for his animal disguises.

By Aztec times sorcery had become partly professionalized. On the one hand, priests seem to have mastered various shamanistic techniques, which they were happy to apply as the occasion demanded in addition to their normal ceremonial duties. On the other, many other individuals seem to have made a living from magical practices.

The greatest demand was for diviners – a role partly filled by the priests who specialized in interpreting the 260-day almanac. Other individuals read the future in the patterns maize grains formed when scattered on a cloak. Fortune-tellers – often old women – would gaze into pots of water or mirrors of polished obsidian in search of clues, and prognosticate the likely outcome of diseases by knotting and unknotting lengths of rope. Some individuals used fasting and hallucinogens to enter trances in which they sought enlightenment. People also consulted spirit healers who claimed to cure ills with the aid of a pharmacopoeia of therapeutic plants alongside various magical techniques shared with North American medicine men. Some apparently used sleight of hand to remove supposed pathogens – typically pebbles or flint blades – from within their patients. Others employed incantations and private rituals as a prelude to "sucking out" the disease.

Entertainers and Illusionists

Public fascination with the supernatural created a demand for illusionists who performed apparently impossible feats as entertainment. Texts are vague about the details of their performances: some apparently were able to swing vessels filled with water from a cord without spilling a drop, but descriptions of others "who toast maize on their mantle", "who burn with flames someone's house" or "who dismember themselves" are less clear. All apparently performed tricks designed to amaze and mystify their audience.

Other *nahualli* had more sinister aims. Black magicians known as "human owls" – a bird of ill omen – sought to bring harm on selected individuals by burning them in effigy or by surreptitiously touching them with blood. "Sleep throwers" carried with them the arm of a woman who had died in childbirth, which was believed to have the power to stupefy all the inhabitants of a house so that they could easily be robbed at night.

The Lady Xoc, in a shamanistic trance, has a vision of a warrior emerging from a serpent's mouth in this Maya stela dated AD725. For reasons unknown, the glyphs are in mirror writing.

The Perilous Journey of the Soul

Mesoamerican ideas about the afterlife were confused and sometimes contradictory, but they shared several traits. One was that most people had little to hope for after death; another was that the progress of the departed soul was a voyage fraught with dangers.

Mesoamericans were for the most part fatalistic in their attitude to death: it came for rich and poor alike, and none could escape it. Aztec poets feelingly compared human life to the fate of a flower or a butterfly, flourishing briefly then swallowed up all too soon. "Our souls in your eyes are but as wisps of smoke or cloud rising out of the earth," one hymn to Tezcatlipoca proclaimed.

Yet distinctions were made between the fortunes awaiting different categories of the dead. The Aztecs and Maya both believed in a multi-tiered world, with thirteen layers rising above the Earth to which the souls of the happy dead might rise, and nine levels below forming an Underworld that was regarded as a sinister place (see pages 24–25). Individuals' destinations in the afterlife were based not on how they had behaved in life, but rather on the manner of their passing. In general, those who died a violent death fared better than those who succumbed to old age or disease. For example, suicides were assigned a place in one of the pleasant upper worlds.

Those who died in battle were also promised a future fit for heroes, at least by the Aztecs. Unlike the rest of the population, who were buried in preparation for a downward journey, war victims were cremated to free the soul for an upward ascent. They could look forward to a happy afterlife sporting as butterflies or hummingbirds in the entourage of the sun. So too could women who died in childbirth, who were similarly seen as casualties, slain in battle with the not-yet-born.

People who drowned, who died of dropsical diseases or who were struck by lightning passed into the realm of the rain god Tlaloc, thought to lie on the fourth level of the upper world. Called Tlalocan, it was visualized as a tropical paradise that the Aztecs – dwellers in dry northern climes – associated with all the pleasures of the south. There, the souls called to the deity sported happily while fruit and flowers blossomed eternally in a perpetual drizzle of warm rain.

A Place of Horrors and Dread

The best that most people could hope for, however, was the Underworld, which for almost all Mesoamerican peoples was looked on with dread. Various creatures were associated with it, particularly the owl, which was regarded as a bird of ill omen. The Maya death god was sometimes represented with an owl's head on a human body. Even today, many people in central America shudder to hear the bird's cry, fearing that it signals a death. Dogs were associated with death, too, though they were conceived more positively as companions on the journey to the Underworld. Some were even sacrificed when their masters died. The concept of the soul's journey after death is attested from both Maya and Aztec sources. To help them on their way, individuals were buried with grave goods that offered sustenance en route. Even the poor would take water and some simple pottery food vessel with them. A jade bead set in the mouth of the corpse served as currency in the Underworld.

The wealthy travelled in more style. The grave of one Maya nobleman at Tikal shows him carried to the tomb on a litter, accompanied by a procession of musicians. Fine ceramics surrounded the body; some of them had contained maize gruel and a frothy chocolate drink for the dead man's refreshment. He had servants to look after him, too, for the remains of nine sacrificial victims were found buried with their master.

The Lord of the Dead, Mictlantecuhtli, took pleasure in others' pain.

The only substantial account of the Maya Underworld to have survived is cited in the *Popul Vuh* (see pages 44–45). The story of the Hero Twins' descent into Xibalba, the Place of Fright, to avenge their father's death chimes with Aztec mythology in portraying the subterranean gods as fearsome and cunning, but ultimately stupid. With patience and alertness, courageous individuals could outwit them.

The story ends with the Twins firmly putting the death gods in their place. "Listen, you Xibalbans," one says; "because of this, your day and your descendants will not be great. Moreover,

The Maya believed that the entrance to the Underworld was through water. To reach it the dead had to undertake an arduous journey, partly by canoe.

127

the gifts you receive will not be great ... just little things broken to pieces." Similar contempt is implied in one Maya title for the principal Underworld deity: Cizin, or "Flatulent One".

Cizin's Aztec equivalent was Mictlantecuhtli, literally "Lord of the Land of the Dead". This dark god was depicted as a figure of horror, a skeleton spotted with flecks of gore wearing vestments of paper, a common offering to the dead. His wife Mictlantecacihuatl, was equally frightful, with a skull for a face, sagging breasts and a skirt of serpents. The couple ruled over the realm of Mictlan, generally thought of as lying in the far north. "It is dark, dark as night, a fearful place, a terrifying place," one text reported. "It is agitating – a frightful thing, a place of ill fortune, without end."

Aztec texts gave more detail about the journey to Mictlan than about the destination itself. The soul's journey after death took it down into the earth, where it first encountered roaring abyssal waters which could only be crossed with the help of a yellow dog. Other horrors waited beyond. There were cliffs that clashed together with the roar of a hundred earthquakes; deserts that had to be crossed, mountains had to be climbed, and monstrous dragons and caimans evaded. Most terrible of all was a land swept by hurricane-force winds in which the freezing air was full of spinning obsidian knives.

The Realm of Mictlan

If the intrepid soul managed to navigate all these menaces, it reached the realm of Mictlan, only to find little comfort awaiting it there. It was stripped of all its accoutrements before simply fading away into oblivion. The journey was thought to take four years, the length of time for which obsequies

Time to Mourn

The Mesoamericans buried their dead with great ceremony, according to Spanish chroniclers. Maya sites have been rich in relics, but the best records are of Aztec rituals.

This vessel in the shape of a turtle with a cormorant on its back, made c.AD350, was found in a Maya tomb.

The Aztecs used two kinds of burial according to an anonymous Spanish conquistador. Most people were cremated, but important nobles were buried in stone vaults. The dead noble would be entombed seated on a chair, with his shield, sword, jewels and gold around him. If he was an important person his wives and servants would be killed when he died so that they could accompany him to the Underworld.

Those who were cremated were tied in a squatting position after being dressed in their best clothes. The body was then swaddled in cloth and decorated with paper and feathers. Then the whole thing was burned.

One of the most curious customs of all was the way children were buried. Their remains have been found within house walls and in yards next to the houses. Even in death children were part of home life. Archaeologists believe that, like modern Mexicans, the Aztecs gave offerings to their dead ancestors.

were paid to the dead. Thereafter all funerary rites ceased, and the rest was silence. Yet, despite the implacable nature of the place the Aztecs, like the Maya, had a myth that told of the outwitting of the Underworld lord. In their case the hero was Quetzalcoatl, who descended to Mictlan after the fourth world had been destroyed (see page 61). His mission was to reclaim the bones of the previous race of fish-men in order to create a new generation of humans.

At first the Underworld lord Mictlantecuhtli pretended to accede to his request for the bones, asking him in return only to perform a simple task: Quetzalcoatl was to travel four times round Mictlan blowing on a conch shell. But the shell had no holes, and made no sound. Quetzalcoatl called on worms to perforate the shell and bees to enter it and make it resound with their humming.

Thwarted, Mictlantecuhtli had to surrender the bones, but prepared a pit to trap Quetzalcoatl, placing a quail in it as a lure. When the bird burst from cover, it so startled the god that he fell in, just as the death lord had planned. However, the chasm proved only a temporary obstacle. The god was able to climb out, retrieving most of the bones, though some had been broken in the fall – a mishap, the Aztecs claimed, that explained why humans were of different sizes. Quetzalcoatl finally succeeded in accomplishing his mission, and the remains he brought back were duly ground up and mixed with the blood of the gods to produce the first people.

Close comparison of this myth with the *Popol Vuh* story has suggested that the two may have more in common than the obvious parallel of a trial of wits with the Underworld's rulers. Study of the iconography of images of One Hunahpu, the father whom the Hero Twins sought to rescue from death, has identified him with the Maya Maize God; the tale of his beheading and subsequent resurrection from the dead thus symbolically replays the germination of fresh

This mask, originally from Teotihuacan but later inlaid by Aztec craftsmen, was used to give a funerary bundle a life-like look.

crops after the annual harvest. Some Maya myths speak of the human race as the people of maize, fashioned from ground corn and blood, suggesting a direct parallel with the Quetzalcoatl story.

Taken together, the two tales suggest a sense of affirmation behind the Mesoamericans' bleak pessimism about the workings of fate. Even if most individuals had little to hope for after death, processes of regeneration were at work on a universal scale that ultimately guaranteed that life itself would continue.

129

DAY OF THE DEAD

One ancient tradition that survived the transition to Christianity was the love of festivals, and today there are almost as many fiestas in Mexico as there were in Aztec times. And no feast more spectacularly combines Christian and pagan elements than the annual Day of the Dead, held every November. Though it nominally marks All Souls Day, this exuberant celebration of human mortality actually harks back in spirit to Mesoamerican times, when ancestors were thought to wield power over the living, inflicting diseases on those who neglected them and serving as intermediaries with the gods. So people today flock to the cemeteries much as they did before the Spanish Conquest, bearing flowers, food and drink both to propitiate and commemorate their departed loved ones.

Left: Death becomes marketable in the run-up to the Day of the Dead when gorgeous papier-maché skeletons decorate department stores.

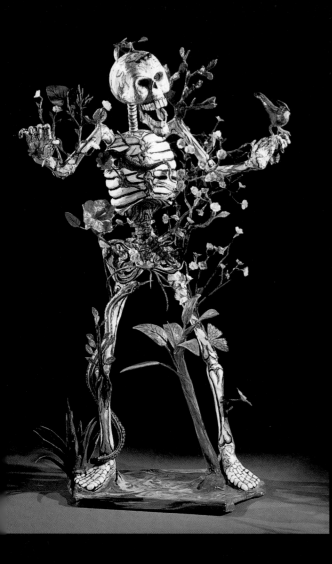

Right: A pottery "Tree of Life" made by Tiburcio Soteno shows an abbreviated version of the human condition, with scenes of baptism, education and courtship on the left and death and burial on the right. The vignette in the top right-hand corner shows an altar decked for the Day of the Dead.

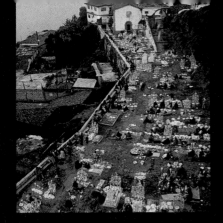

Right: Dusk falls on families celebrating the Day of the Dead in a Mexican cemetery. Traditionally, tombs are swept and cleaned, candles are lit and portraits of the deceased are prominently displayed.

Above: The skeletal Aztec deity Mictlantecuhtli sits back-to-back with his divine adversary Quetzalcoatl in a detail from the *Codex Borgia*. Mesoamerican death gods were held in a spirit of sometimes mocking familiarity that finds an echo in the modern festivities.

Right: Death and the devil dance a slow salsa. This type of colourfully macabre object is sold all over Mexico in the lead up to the Day of the Dead.

THE MESOAMERICAN LEGACY

After being ignored or reviled for hundreds of years after the Spanish Conquest, Mesoamerican culture eventually became a source of pride for the people of the region. A series of extraordinary archaeological finds at the end of the eighteenth century stimulated interest, and by the beginning of this century, the pre-Colombian heritage had become a cornerstone of national identity.

For the Mesoamerican peoples, the results of the Spanish Conquest were calamitous. The great and glorious city of Tenochtitlan itself was largely destroyed in the fighting, and what was left was subsequently razed to provide building materials for the new Spanish capital. The citizens could only look on in stunned despair as their treasured monuments were broken and dismantled.

For 200 years following the Conquest, the situation of the Indians was wretched indeed. Some learned Spanish and intermingled with the incomers to form a growing *mestizo* (mixed-blood) population, but the rest became firmly stuck at the bottom of the colonial social ladder.

New agricultural methods, including the introduction of draught animals, did bring economic benefits, but few of these found their way to the Indians. By the end of the eighteenth century, it was estimated that Indians made up between half and two-thirds of Mexico's population, yet owned almost none of its wealth. Even so, the damage done to the native population by

In the 19th century Alfred P. Maudslay's photographs of ancient Maya sites brought the marvels of Mesoamerican history to a wider audience. This photograph shows him at work in a makeshift study somewhere in Central America.

exploitation was small compared to the ravages wrought by disease. Sheltered by their long isolation, the Indians had no immunity to many ailments that had long been endemic across the Eurasian landmass. The result was that conditions such as measles and influenza, which were little more than irritants to the Spanish settlers, proved fatal to the Indians. As a result of epidemics of these diseases and also of smallpox, the population of Mexico declined from upwards of 11 million in 1519 to barely 1.5 million by 1650. Even though levels of population gradually rose again as immunities were eventually acquired, they never, in colonial times, came close to those of Aztec days.

But by the end of the eighteenth century, changes were under way beneath the surface of colonial life that were eventually to transform the situation. The ideas of the Enlightenment slowly made their way across the Atlantic, affecting firstly attitudes towards Mesoamerican antiquities. So when the 24-ton Calendar Stone – now the most treasured exhibit in Mexico City's National

Museum of Anthropology – was unearthed in 1790 beneath the city's main square, it was not smashed as it would no doubt have been a couple of hundred years before; instead, it was studied by scholars before being put on display against a wall of the city's cathedral (see page 114).

The nineteenth century saw the beginnings of serious archaeological investigation of Mesoamerican remains. The pioneering work was done by a handful of scholar-explorers who set off into the jungles of Guatemala and the Yucatán and discovered wonders unknown to Europeans. So John L. Stephens, an American diplomat, and his travelling companion, the British artist Frederick Catherwood, risked their lives visiting and describing such sites as Palenque, Uxmal and Copán in 1839–40 when much of Central America was engulfed in civil war. A half a century later, the

archaeologist, Alfred P. Maudslay spent thirteen years recording the remains of ancient life, providing volumes of source materials for the study of Maya writing and religion.

Seeds of Revolution

After the Conquest, Cortés distributed Aztec lands to his followers in the form of *encomiendas* – literally, "entrustments". In theory the new Spanish masters were supposed to look after the Indians in their care in return for free labour and an annual tribute of food and goods. In practice, they usually

Diego Rivera's colourful mural shows Mesoamericans dying cloth. The communal engagement depicted in this work celebrates values contrary to those of the land-owning hierarchies imposed after the Spanish Conquest.

Emiliano Zapata stands stoically in this 1913 photograph. The charismatic revolutionary leader gained huge popularity among the peasantry because of his land reforms.

sought to improve their own standard of living by ruthlessly exploiting their charges. And despite the sporadic efforts of royal appointees sent from the mother country, nobody in the ruling establishment had the means or the inclination to prevent them.

The Indians' political situation only started to improve with the ending of colonial rule. Benito Juárez, the president who eventually restored order to Mexico after the chaotic early decades of the Republic, was himself a full-blooded Zapotec.

Yet the peasantry remained severely disadvantaged, trapped in a cycle of debt and servitude to the large estate-owners. As a result, Indians fighting under the banner of "Land and Liberty" made up the bulk of the guerrilla forces led by Emiliano Zapata and Pancho Villa in the Mexican Revolution of the 1910s. Zapata's treatment of the rich was ruthless: he burned haciendas and ordered executions. Yet he believed passionately in fairness. During his occupation of certain areas of Mexico, he redistributed land and supported the poor peasantry by taxing the cities. He also attempted to organize the sugar industry into co-operatives and set up Mexico's first rural bank to lend money to peasants. After Zapata was assassinated by followers of Venustiano Carranza (the self-appointed president) in 1917, agrarian reform slowed down.

Artistic Renaissance

One result of the revolution was a marked shift in attitude towards the Mesoamerican past. Mexico's early civilizations were held up as a model, while the colonial inheritance was largely decried. The new pride in the ancient cultures was especially strong in the artistic community. One artist who was to become head of the government's Department of Fine Arts even changed his last name from Murillo to Atl – the Nahuatl word for water – to signal his allegiance to the Aztec world.

It was a time of public art in the young Republic, and the leading practitioners shared the enthusiasm of Dr Atl. The most famous of them all, the painter Diego Rivera, sometimes hired buses to take wild trips with friends into the countryside in search of Mesoamerican monuments, drinking quantities of tequila and firing off pistols on the way. Rivera also became an avid collector of pre-Columbian works; his collection was only slightly diminished on the occasion when the second of his four wives – Frida Kahlo – smashed one treasured pot and served up the shards in his soup.

Rivera's fellow-muralists, José Orozco and David Siqueiros, also learned from their Mesoamerican predecessors. It was symbolic of the time that when Orozco's work ignited controversy, it was for including a scene suggesting that the Conquest had in fact had some beneficial effects. Students at the National Preparatory School in Mexico City, where the mural was painted, were so outraged at this affront to the new orthodoxy that they pelted the work with stones, eggs and fruit, and it consequently had to be boarded up for its own protection.

A Mexican interpretation of the Last Supper retains ties to the ancestral Indian culture through the stylistic treatment of its Christian iconography. The craftsmanship preserves the Mesoamerican artistic tradition of bold linear patterns, bright flat colours and abstract rendering of figures.

But perhaps the artist who most clearly owed a debt to her Mesoamerican roots was Diego Rivera's wife Frida Kahlo. Like her husband, Kahlo found inspiration in the history of her native land, but she explored Mexican identity from a more personal perspective. In contrast to the scale and overt political aims of her male contemporaries, Kahlo's works were small and highly personal. Her surrealist self-portraits managed to combine Christian and pre-Columbian iconography with verve and originality. For many years the overt – and very Aztec – goriness of her work offended critics. But in the mid-1980s, Kahlo's work was rediscovered, and art historians have given her a significant place in twentieth century art.

But to many observers – academics, tourists and the people of the region themselves – the most important inheritance from the pre-Columbian world is religious. After the Conquest, a priority for the Spanish was to convert the local population to Catholicism – a task that was made easier by the apparent disfavour of the Mesoamerican gods. If any emotion rivalled greed among the Spanish settlers, it was the conviction of their own religion's absolute superiority to the blood-drenched worship it supplanted. Once the lands of Central America had formally passed to the Spanish crown, it became government policy to save the souls of the king's new subjects.

However, old customs and beliefs survived despite the best efforts of the small army of priests who arrived from Spain intent on bringing the

135

gospel to the new lands. For most of the new-comers, relics of the old Mesoamerican beliefs were quite simply demonic, and they eagerly set about extirpating all trace of them. One bishop boasted of having destroyed 500 temples and broken up 20,000 idols. Another, Diego de Landa, studied local customs in the Yucatán peninsula and prepared a valuable work describing them; yet he too was surprised to find that the Maya were more than a little upset to see the Spaniards burning their splendid collections of books.

In fact, relatively little compulsion was required. Used to reading the will of the gods in the course of events, the Indians simply combined Christianity with the old faith, creating a unique religion, Mexican Catholicism. Some ancient rituals continued to be performed surreptitiously. Relics of the gods were placed in the foundations of the new churches being built by the Spanish. Old rituals were moved to Christian dates, for example the annual visiting of graves now took place on All Soul's Day. And the local population took to the host of Catholic saints with a passion. The Mesoamericans simply identified their own gods with specific saints; for example, Tlaloc was linked with St John the Baptist. Most famously perhaps, a dark-complexioned Virgin Mary appeared to the peasant Juan Diego a few years after the Conquest – outside the temple to the earth goddess Tonantzin. Known as the Black Virgin of Guadalupe, she is now the patron saint of Mexico.

A classic anthropological study of the Tzotzil of Zinacantan – a mountainous region on Mexico's southern border – found a fascinating blending of faiths. The team from Harvard University that studied them reported that the 12,000-strong community conceived of the world as having four corners, each borne on the shoulders of a god; a mound of earth in a centrally located ceremonial site represented its mid-point. Earthquakes were thought to occur when one of the corner gods slipped.

The Indians addressed the Sun as "Our Holy Father" and associated it with God and Jesus Christ; the Virgin Mary was identified with the Moon. Although great veneration was paid to statues of Catholic saints, rituals involving offerings of chickens, incense and alcohol were also performed in honour of ancestral deities thought to live in the surrounding mountains. St Sebastian was an important figure in the Tzotzil pantheon, but so was the Earth Lord, held to control lightning and rain and thought of as greedy, fat and – in a reflection of prevailing social attitudes – Spanish.

Mexicans dressed as Aztecs celebrate the feast of the Virgin of Guadalupe. The unique blend of pagan and Christian elements is partly the result of Spanish missionaries eventually encouraging the Mesoamericans to make associations between Christian figures and their own deities as a way of understanding concepts from the Bible.

A Question of Identity

Nearly 500 years after the Conquest of Central America, its indigenous people are still struggling to assert their identity – both politically and culturally.

In the hills of Guatemala and Mexico, isolated communities keep alive traditions from Aztec and ancestral Maya times. Social conditions for such groups, as for the peasantry at large, continue to cause concern, and on occasion discontent has burst out into revolt. Maya communities were deeply involved in both the Guatemalan insurgency of the 1980s and the Zapatista uprising in southern Mexico in the 1990s. The former had particularly dire consequences; an estimated 190,000 Maya died in the course of counter-insurgency operations by the Guatemalan army, and a further one million were made homeless out of an estimated total population of three million.

Since then, however, there are signs that the situation has improved. The struggle for recognition of Maya rights received worldwide publicity when the human rights activist Rigoberta Menchu received the Nobel Peace Prize in 1992 for her

Despite death threats, exile and the execution of her family, Nobel laureate Rigoberta Menchu continues to publicize the plight of her people, the Maya.

efforts to stop the oppression and silencing of Indians. Despite the execution of her family, Menchu has continued to plead for social justice. Her campaign for the recognition of the indigenous peoples' condition has generated international concern over the Guatemalan government's disregard for human rights.

Pride in ancestry

Since the 1930s, appreciation and knowledge of Mesoamerican art has spread out to widening sections of the population, not just in Mexico but also in neighbouring countries, particularly Guatemala. In recent years Maya culture has increasingly made its presence felt in mass culture. Today tales from the *Popol Vuh* turn up in comic strips that themselves borrow graphic elements from the ancient codices. The old glyphs find their way onto commemorative plaques, and diaries featuring the 260-day calendar have become popular.

The region's archaeological heritage is even more widely admired. Visitors stream out of Mexico City at weekends to marvel at the splendours of Teotihuacan, and tourists from around the world crowd such sites as Monte Albán and Chichen Itza, Palenque, Bonampak and Copán.

New discoveries continue to be made regularly, not least in Mexico City itself, where every large public-work excavation seems to turn up yet another reminder of Tenochtitlan, the old Aztec capital buried beneath its streets.

In cultural terms, appreciation of the Mesoamerican achievement continues to spread, a process that can only be accelerated by the recent decipherment of Mayan writings. Those new to the heritage of Mesoamerica may come to share the excitement of one early witness, the German artist Albrecht Dürer, almost four centuries ago. "I have seen nothing that has so rejoiced my heart as these things," he wrote in his journal after seeing Aztec artefacts sent back by Cortés to the Emperor Charles V, "for I saw in them strange and exquisitely worked objects, and marvelled at the subtle genius of men in distant lands."

The Calendar

The Months of the 365-day Aztec Calendar

The 365-day calendar of the Aztecs followed the seasons – beginning with the planting of the seed corn. Every month particular deities, family or ancestors were honoured and special rituals were performed. Dates are approximate.

Date and Name

Those Honoured and Rituals Observed

February 14-March 5. Ceasing of Water

Tlaloc. Children were sacrificed over water.

March 6-25. Flaying of Men

Xipe Topec. Victims were sacrificed at temples; then flayed and their skins worn by priests.

March 26-April 13. Little Vigil

Tlaloc, Cinteotl, Chalchihuitlicue, Chicomecoatl. Skins from the previous month were discarded and seeds were planted.

April 14-May 3. Great Vigil

Cinteotl, Chicomecoatl, Tlaloc, Quetzalcoatl. Maize stalks were woven into representations of gods and brought into the home.

May 4-22. Dryness

Tezcatlipoca, Huitzilopochtli. Tezcatlipoca's human impersonator was sacrificed.

May 23-June 13. Eating of the Maize Bean Porridge

Tlaloc, Chalchihuitlicue, Quetzalcoatl. Hearts and gems were offered to Tlaloc.

June 14-July 3. Little Feast of the Lords

Xochipilli, Uixtocihuatl. Women danced and donned skirts decorated with conch shells.

July 4-23. Great Feast of the Lords

Xilonen, Cihuacoatl. Warriors had intercourse with "pleasure girls" who were then sacrificed. Drunkards may have been executed.

July 24-August 12. Offerings of Flowers
(Little Feast of the Dead)

Ancestors, Huitzilopochtli, Tezcatlipoca, all gods in general. Flowers were offered to icons.

August 13-September 1. The Fruit Falls
(Great Feast of the Dead)

Xiuhticuhtli, Huehueteotl. Fire sacrifices were made. Boys competed to climb an enormous pole representing the World Tree.

September 2-21. The Sweeping

Teteo Innan, Toci, Cinteotl, Chicomecoatl. Teteo Innan's human impersonator was sacrificed; corn harvested and the season of war inaugurated.

September 22-October 11. The Gods Arrive

All the gods. Dancing, singing and feasting.

October 12-October 31. The Feast of the Mountain

Tlaloc, Xochiquetzal, gods of pulque. Miniature dough mountains were made. Dough and human flesh were then eaten.

November 1-20. Precious Feather

Mixcoatl, the dead. All the men went on a communal hunt and camped out.

November 21-December 10. The Raising of the Banners

Huitzilopochtli, Tezcatlipoca. Merchants offered "bathed slaves".

December 11-30. The Descent of Water

Tlaloc. Young priests and warriors fought.

December 31-January 19. The Stretching

Cihuacoatl, Tonantzin. Tonantzin's impersonator was sacrificed; then the priest danced with her severed head.

January 20-February 8. Growth, Rebirth

Family and relatives, Xiuhtecuhtli, Tlaloc, Chalchihuitlicue. Lots of pulque was drunk.

February 9-13. The Barren Days

People fasted and stayed indoors waiting for the evil time to pass.

The Day-signs of the 260-day Calendar

A religious 260-day calendar was used by all Mesoamericans (see pages 114–117) alongside the 365-day solar calendar. Some highland Maya and some Oaxacan peoples still use it today. There are twenty day names, each associated with one or two incarnations of a deity. Each name-day would be added to a number from one to thirteen in rotation until the 260th day was reached and then the cycle would all start again. So the year began One Alligator, Two Wind, Three House and so on. The deities associated with the first nine day-names are also associated with the nine lords of the night. These day names and deities are from the Nahuatl calendar.

Day name	Deity (Nahuatl)	Deity (English)
Alligator	Xochipilli/Tonacatecuhtli	Prince of Flowers/Supreme Male Deity
Wind	Quetzalcoatl/Ehecatl	Plumed Serpent/Wind God
House	Tezcatlipoca as Tepeyollotl	Heart of Mountain
Lizard	Huehuecoyotl	Old Coyote
Serpent	Chalchiuhtlicue	She of the Jade Skirt/Goddess of Running Water
Death	Teciztecatl	Moon Goddess
Deer	Tlaloc	God of Rain and Storm
Rabbit	Mayahuel	Goddess of the Maguey Cactus
Water	Xiuhtecuhtli/Red Tezcatlipoca	God of Fire
Dog	Mictlantecuhtli	God of the Underworld
Monkey	Xochipilli	Prince of Flowers
Grass	Patecatl/One Rabbit	God of Pulque
Reed	Tezcatlipoca as Ixquimilli	The Smoking Mirror with Bandaged Eyes
Jaguar	Tlazolteotl	Goddess of Filth
Eagle	Xipe Totec	The Flayed Lord
Vulture	Itzpapalotl	Obsidian Butterfly
Movement	Xolotl	God of Twins
Flint	Chalchiuhtotolin	Turkey of the Precious Stone
Rain	Tonatiuh	Sun
Flower	Xochiquetzal	Precious Flower

Pronunciation guide

Spelling of Maya and Nahuatl words for the most part follows Spanish rules, because these languages were first transliterated into Roman script by the conquistadors.
In Nahuatl, the language of the Aztecs, the accent is usually put on the penultimate syllable, for example Huitzilopótchli or Coatlícue. The Maya usually put the emphasis on the last syllable, for example Copán or Tikál.

Vowels are pronounced in the Spanish way. Each vowel is pronounced separately:

a is like **a** in father.
e is like **e** in prey and is always sounded, so for example, Coatlicue is pronounced Ko-at-lee-kway.
i is long like the double **ee** in bee or knee.
o is like **o** in open or oaf.
u is the like the double **o** in zoo.

Consonants are pronounced similarly to English with some exceptions.

h is pronounced **hw**.
c is always hard in Maya. In Nahuatl, it is soft before e or i, hard before o, a or u. For example Cipactonal is pronounced See-pak-to-nal.

ch is pronounced like **ch** in charge.
qua and **quo** are pronounced **kw**.
que and **qui** are pronounced **k**.
tl is pronounced like **tl** in atlas.
tz is hissed hard against the back of the teeth.
x is pronounced **sh**.
z is pronounced **s** as in sad.
j is pronounced like the English **h** as in hat.

Some examples are:
Quetzalcoatl – Ke-tsal-co-atl
Huitzilopochtli – Hweets-il-oe-poch-tli
Xipe Totec – Shee-pay Toe-tec
Chalchiuhtlicue – Chall-chee-wit-lee-kway
Xochipilli – Sho-chee-pee-lee
Xolotl – Sho-lotl
Xochiquetzal – Sho-chee-ketz-all

Index

Further Reading

Boone, Elizabeth Hill, *The Aztec World, Exploring the Ancient World*, Smithsonian Institute, Washington D.C., 1982.

Carter, Geraldine, *The Illustrated Guide to Latin American Mythology*, Studio Editions, London, 1995.

Coe, Michael D., *The Maya*, Thames and Hudson, 4th Ed, London, 1993.

Coe, Michael D., *Mexico: From the Olmecs to the Aztecs*, Thames and Hudson, London, 1994.

Coe, Michael D., *Lords of the Underworld*, Princeton, 1978.

Miller, Mary Ellen, *The Art of Mesoamerica: From Olmec to Aztec*, Thames and Hudson, World of Art Series, London, 1996.

Miller, Mary Ellen and Schele, Linda, *The Blood of Kings*, George Braziller, New York, 1985.

Miller, Mary and Taube, Karl, *The Gods and Symbols of Ancient Mexico and the Maya, An Illustrated Dictionary of Mesoamerican Religion*, Thames and Hudson, London, 1993.

Morley, Sylvanus, *The Ancient Maya*, editor Robert L. Sharer, Stanford University Press, California, 1983.

Nicholson, H.B., "Religion in Pre-Hispanic Mexico", *Handbook of Middle American Indians*, volume 10, Los Angeles, 1971.

Stephens, John Lloyd, *Incidents of Travel in Central America, Chiapas and Yucatán*, 2 volumes, New York, 1841.

Stephens, John Lloyd, *Incidents of Travel in Yucatán*, 2 vols, New York, 1843.

Stuart, George E. and Gene S., *The Mysterious Maya*, National Geographic Society, Washington D.C., 1977.

Taube, Karl, *Aztec and Maya Myths*, British Museum Press, London, 1995.

Townsend, Richard, *The Aztecs*, Thames and Hudson, London, 1992.

Wauchope, Robert et al, ed. *Handbook of Middle American Indians*, 16 volumes and five supplements, University of Texas, 1964–1995.

Weaver, Muriel Porter, *The Aztecs, the Maya and their Predecessors: Archaeology of Mesoamerica*, Academic Press, New York, 1981.

Whitecotton, Joseph, *The Zapotecs*, University of Oklahoma Press, 1977.

Some Primary Sources

Duran, Fray Diego, *Book of the Gods and Rites (Codex Duran)*, trans. Horcasitas, F. and Hayden, D., New York, 1964.

Popol Vuh, trans. Tedlock, D., Simon and Schuster, New York, 1985.

Sahagún, Fray Bernardino de, *The Florentine Codex: A General History of the Things of New Spain*, trans. A.J.O. Anderson and C.E. Dibble, Santa Fé, 1950–82.

Picture Credits

The publishers wish to thank the photographers and organizations for their kind permission to reproduce the following illustrations in this book:

Key: t top; **b** bottom; **c** centre; **l** left; **r** right

BAL:	Bridgeman Art Library
BL:	British Library
BM:	British Museum

et:	e.t. Archive
MAM:	Museum of Anthropology, Mexico City
JDK:	Justin and Deborah Kerr
WFA:	Werner Forman Archive

5 JDK; **6** BAL/BL; **7** et; **9** WFA/Liverpool Museum; **11** Images Colour Library; **12l** WFA/MAM; **12r** South American Pictures; **13f** WFA/Liverpool Museum; **13bl** Tony Stone Images/Richard Cooke III; **13br** BAL; **14** et; **15** WFA/BM; **16** South American Pictures/Chris Sharp; **17** WFA/Museum für Volkerkunde, Basel; **18** et/National Library, Mexico; **19** WFA; 20tr WFA/Dallas Museum of Art, USA; **20c** BAL/BM; **20b** WFA/Dallas Museum of Art; **21l** Tony Stone Images/Susanne Murphy; **21tr** WFA; **21br** WFA; **22** JDK; **23** South American Pictures; **24** JDK; **25** JDK; **26** BAL; **27** Princeton University Libraries, USA; **28** South American Pictures; **29c** Newberry Library, Chicago, USA; **29b** JDK; **30** JDK; **32** JDK; **33** JDK; **34** WFA; **35** JDK; **36** JDK; **37** JDK; **38** JDK; **40** JDK; **41** South American Pictures/Chris Sharp; **42** JDK; **43** JDK: **44** JDK; **45** JDK; **47** JDK; **48** WFA; **49** JDK; **50** JDK; **51** JDK; **52** Robert Harding Picture Library; **53** BAL; **54tr** National Geographic Society/Doug Stern & Enrico Fererelli; **54** National Geographic Society/Doug Stern & Enrico Fererelli; **54bl** Andes Press Agency; **55tl, tr, b** National Geographic Society/ Doug Stern & Enrico Fererelli; **56** Michael Holford; **57** Tony Stone Images/Richard Cooke III; **58** WFA/Museum für Volkerkunde, Basel; **59** Newberry Library, Chicago; **60** WFA/MAM; **61** et; **62** et; **63** WFA/MAM; **64** Codex Borgia; **65** John B. Taylor; **66** et/National Library, Mexico; **68** Jean-Loup Charmet; **70–71** WFA/BM; **73** Codex Borgia/DBP; **74** et; **75** BAL/BM; **76** Tony Stone Images/Robert Frerck; **77** WFA/MAM; **80t** South American Pictures/Robert Francis; **80–81b** Tony Stone Images/Cosmo Condina; **81tl, tr** South American Pictures/Robert Francis; **81** Tony Stone Images; **82** et; **83** WFA/MAM; **85** South American Pictures; **86** et/MAM; **87** WFA/BM; **88** WFA; **89** et/National Library Mexico; **91** BAL/BM; **92** Dr Peter Furst; **93** Codex Nuttall-Zouche/DBP **94** Gabriel Flores Figueroa; **95** DBP Archives; **96** John B. Taylor; **97** Codex Borgia/DBP; **99** et/National Library, Mexico; **101** Gabriel Flores Figueroa; **103** WFA/Liverpool Museum; **104** WFA/Volkerkunde Museum, Berlin, Germany; **105** et/National Library, Mexico; **106** BAL/Bibliotheque Medicae Laurenziano, Florence; **107** WFA/Anthropology Museum, Veracruz University, Veracruz, Mexico; **108** WFA/Volkerkunde Museum, Berlin; **110l** Nicholas Saunders; **110–111** Chris Caldicott; **111tl** South American Pictures; **111tr, b** Zefa Pictures; **112** BAL/Bibliotheque Apostolica Vaticana; **113** Chloe Sayer; **114** WFA; **115** JDK; **116** WFA; **118** WFA/MAM; **119** WFA/Volkerkunde Museum, Berlin; **120** et; **121** JDK; **123** Bibliotheque de l'Assemblée de Paris; **125** JDK; **127** WFA; **128** JDK; **129** Images Colour Library; **130** Museum of Mankind; **130–131** Museum of Mankind; **131t** Tony Stone Images; **131c** DBP Archives; **131b** Museum of Mankind; **132** Royal Geographical Society; **133** BAL/National Palace, Mexico City; **134** Popperfoto; **135** Robert Harding Picture Library; **136** South American Pictures; **137** Frank Spooner Picture Agency